Walter Rodney

THE CARIBBEAN BIOGRAPHY SERIES

The Caribbean Biography Series from the University of the West Indies Press celebrates and memorializes the architects of Caribbean culture. The series aims to introduce general readers to those individuals who have made sterling contributions to the region in their chosen field – literature, the arts, politics, sports – and are the shapers and bearers of Caribbean identity.

Series Editor: Funso Aiyejina

Other Titles in This Series

Earl Lovelace, by Funso Aiyejina
Derek Walcott, by Edward Baugh
Marcus Garvey, by Rupert Lewis
Beryl McBurnie, by Judy Raymond
Una Marson, by Lisa Tomlinson
Stuart Hall, by Annie Paul
Lucille Mathurin Mair, by Verene Shepherd
Aimé Césaire, by Elizabeth Walcott-Hackshaw

WALTER RODNEY

Rupert Lewis

The University of the West Indies Press
Mona • St Augustine • Cave Hill • Global • Five Islands

The University of the West Indies Press
7A Gibraltar Hall Road, Mona
Kingston 7, Jamaica
www.uwipress.com

A catalogue record of this book is
available from the National Library of Jamaica.
ISBN: 978-976-640-927-2 (cloth)
978-976-640-928-9 (paper)
978-976-640-950-0 (ePub)
978-976-640-951-7 (audio)

Cover photograph reproduced by kind courtesy
of the Walter Rodney Foundation
Jacket and book design by Robert Harris
Set in Whitman 11.5/15
Printed in the United States of America

CONTENTS

INTRODUCTION

Among the critical questions that Rodney dealt with, whether he was in Tanzania, Jamaica or his native Guyana (formerly British Guiana) was the character of the postcolonial state and its relationship with the working people. It is his engagement with politics which guided his research into African and Caribbean history. In the post–Second World War era, the colonial powers had regrouped and were rebuilding Europe with the strong financial and political support of the capitalist United States. The Soviet Union, one of the victors over German fascism, was the other power on the world scene. It was communist and engaged in a Cold War with the United States, the dominant global power. China under Mao Tse Tung was the other communist state, with a huge rural population, much poverty and a low level of industrialization that had emerged after the 1949 revolution. Capitalist and socialist powers vied for the hearts and minds of the peoples of Asia, Africa and the Caribbean who were shaking off the shackles of colonialism. Latin American countries which had achieved their political independence in the nineteenth century were caught up in this nationalist

INTRODUCTION

surge as they battled with neocolonialism. They battled with
Spain their colonial overlord and with the United States, which
regarded Latin America and the Caribbean as its backyard and
intervened as it saw fit to pursue its strategic military, political
and economic goals.

The Garvey and labour movements of the 1920s and 1930s
in the Caribbean as well as communist and national liberation
movements in the twentieth century helped to shape Walter
Rodney's political awareness. His parents' generation was
actively involved in the anti-colonial movement in British
Guiana in the 1940s and 1950s; and in the 1960s and 1970s,
Rodney himself helped to shape the ideas around African and
Caribbean decolonization, Pan-Africanism and Marxism.

To understand his political world, one must know the
varieties of movements in which he was engaged in Africa
and the Caribbean, his support for Black Power in the United
States and Europe and his advocacy for socialist movements.
The 1960s and 1970s saw the emergence of social and
political movements in the region, covering a wide range of
social, economic, cultural and political ideas. Walter Rodney
represented the revolutionary wing of decolonization.

He contributed to the development of Marxist theory in the
1960s and 1970s by applying this tool of analysis to the history
of Africa and the Caribbean. He was a leader in transformative
teaching methods and political work in Tanzania and in the
Caribbean, especially in Guyana from 1974 to 1980. His
contribution to political education occurred in communities
of working people through study groups organized in schools,
churches, work sites and universities.

ONE

Rodney grew up in the context of the struggles of the people of British Guiana to free their country from colonial rule. His parents were supporters of the People's Progressive Party (PPP) led by Dr Cheddi Jagan, an Indian dentist, and for a brief period until the British occupation of 1953, the possibility loomed of a political movement uniting both Africans and Indians in a political struggle for freedom.[1] Dr Cheddi Jagan's People's Progressive Party (PPP) won eighteen of the twenty-four seats to the Legislative Council. Cheddi Jagan's administration included the African Forbes Burnham, minister of education, and Sydney King, minister of communications and works. But after 133 days, the British brought in the warships and suspended the constitution, thereby staging a coup d'état against a democratically elected government. With the support of the United States, the British alleged that this new government was a communist regime led by Dr Jagan. The British thus fractured the political compact that underlay the attempt at racial unity in the anti-colonial struggle. This fracture has ever since been at the heart of the racial polarity in the politics of Guyana. Walter Rodney was among those political activists in the 1970s committed to bringing about political co-operation among working people across racial lines.

As a young boy, Rodney recalled distributing the manifesto of the PPP. He therefore was politically socialized in the radical anti-colonial politics of the 1950s. Walter Rodney's father was Edward Percival Rodney, a tailor, and his mother, Pauline, a homemaker. She gave birth to six children, five boys and a girl. Walter was the second child. It was a humble Afro-Guyanese household in the capital city, Georgetown.

The population comprised descendants of enslaved Africans and Indian indentured labourers. Indentureship had only ended in 1917. Slavery had been abolished in 1838. Other components of the population included the marginalized indigenous Amerindians, in addition to Portuguese and Chinese. All these peoples were ruled by British colonial officials. A plantation economy dominated this British colony in South America, with a large sugar plantation working class. But mining in bauxite, gold and diamonds provided alternative occupations for the working class, in addition to peasant farming.

Political tensions within the PPP arose between Forbes Burnham and Cheddi Jagan over political leadership, with the British and Americans opposed to Jagan and his American-born wife, Janet, because of their left-wing views. Janet Jagan was herself general secretary of the PPP and editor of the party monthly, *Thunder*. An American white woman born to Jewish parents, her maiden name was Rosenberg. Forbes Burnham, whose base was the African-Guyanese population, had the support of the United States and Britain because he was assessed as someone they could collaborate with. Burnham emerged as a leader of the predominantly African-based Peoples' National Congress and would lead Guyana to independence in 1966 and make Guyana a Cooperative Republic in 1970. He would rig elections to stay in power. Burnham became prime minister in 1966 when Guyana got independence from Britain and in 1980 became president until his death in 1985.

As a schoolboy in the 1950s, Rodney recognized that "there was a whole generation of already adult young Guyanese – the Martin Carters and so on – who were participating in the political events of 1953, and who were extremely creative and extremely revolutionary at the same time".[2] Carter's revolutionary poetry and journalism reflected the radical age of Caribbean anti-colonialism. Carter's *Poems of Resistance* was written in his early twenties after the 1953 actions by the British. Sydney King, who later adopted the name Eusi Kwayana, would, in the 1970s, become a mentor to Walter Rodney and encourage him to return to Guyana from Tanzania. Kwayana, a teacher and political activist, along with young intellectuals such as Rupert Roopnarine, filmmaker and literary critic, and Andaiye, who would emerge as a formidable Caribbean feminist activist and thinker, would co-lead the Working People's Alliance. Andaiye, originally Sandra Williams, whose political evolution paralleled Walter's, explained:

> Each stage of my political life started with a sense of being discriminated against in a particular place – as a citizen of a colony, for instance, or as a person of African descent; and my

politics were informed first by a kind of Guyanese/West Indian nationalism, later of ideas of the Black Power movement, then by Marxism. What was consistent throughout this journey was a search for explanations of how power worked and, increasingly, of how each power relation worked in interaction with others.[3]

Rodney attended Queen's College, the premier boys' high school in British Guiana, from 1953 to 1960. Robert 'Bobby' Moore, his history teacher, used the lectures of Dr Elsa Goveia at UCWI (University College of the West Indies, then attached to the University of London), Jamaica, to teach West Indian history, thus breaking from the traditional history of the British Empire offered in the high school programme. Rodney's brilliance as a debater, and his superb analytical skills were evident, so he was among a group of bright boys who excelled academically. A generation before, Cheddi Jagan and Forbes Burnham had both graduated from Queen's College. As such, the teachers and students in this colonial school were at the time preparing a Guyanese intellectual and political leadership group that would succeed the British. But the thinking among some graduates was geared towards decolonization, not the continuation of British colonialism. Among the graduates of Rodney's generation were Rupert Roopnarine, who was a Guyanese scholar to Cambridge University, and who became co-leader of the Working People's Alliance. Another was Ewart Thomas, a gifted mathematician and University of the West Indies (UWI) graduate who went on to a career as a professor at Stanford University and who wrote the preface to the first edition of *Groundings with My Brothers*. Yet another close friend was Gordon Rohlehr who attended the UWI, Mona, Jamaica, and the University of Birmingham,

England, and lectured at the University of the West Indies, St Augustine campus in Trinidad, becoming a creative assessor of Caribbean postcolonial literature and calypso, contributing essays in this vein to radical publications such as *Moko,* founded by James Millette, and *Tapia*, later renamed *Trinidad and Tobago Review,* founded by Lloyd Best.

Queen's College thus laid the foundation for Rodney's intellectual formation as a radical thinker, sharp-witted debater and writer. His years at UWI added value to his research capabilities and honed his writing and debating skills. At UWI from 1960 to 1963, he studied history under Elsa Goveia, Roy Augier and Douglas Hall. But he also was actively involved in the campaign for the West Indian Federation in 1961, when Jamaica voted to abandon the Federation. He also visited Cuba and attended a student conference in the Soviet Union. These visits brought him to the attention of Special Branch in Kingston, Jamaica, and his name was added to the list of subversive radicals.

At the University of the West Indies in Jamaica, he gained a first-class honours bachelor of arts degree in history in 1963. He won a scholarship to do his PhD at the School of Oriental and African Studies at the University of London in 1966 and completed his thesis "A History of the Upper Guinea Coast, 1545–1800" at twenty-four years old. He then taught at the University of Dar es Salaam in 1966 during the period of radical political and agrarian reform in Tanzania, under the leadership of President Julius Nyerere. Tanzania was the headquarters of the Organization of African Unity's Liberation Committee. Dar es Salaam therefore became the base for the exiled liberation movements of Southern Africa. Among these organizations were the African National Congress (ANC) of South Africa, FRELIMO of Mozambique and MPLA of Angola. In this atmosphere, Rodney developed his Pan-African perspectives along Marxist lines and sided with Southern Africa's left-wing activists. When he returned to Jamaica to teach at the University of the West Indies in 1968, he not only had expert knowledge on West African history but had also studied East African history. In addition, he had a good grasp of the economic, ethnic as well as the social and cultural developmental challenges facing Africa. With his academic credentials in African history and his knowledge of contemporary Africa, he established a reputation as a lecturer and speaker not only on the campus of UWI but also in the wider community. Rodney was both a Marxist and Black Power advocate, with links to communities of the poor and young Rastafarians. But the neocolonial state in Jamaica was fearful of the potential for grass-roots mobilization inspired by the black consciousness that Rastafari activists had done so much to stimulate.

Rodney's association with Rastafarians and the Black Power movement in Jamaica led to Prime Minister Hugh Shearer imposing a ban on him from re-entering Jamaica, after he attended a Black Writers' conference in Montreal, Canada, on 15 October 1968. On 16 October 1968, a demonstration of university students together with Kingston's urban youth against this ban marked a watershed in Jamaica's political development, as the scale of mass action in Rodney's support surprised the Jamaican regime. In addition, there were protests throughout the Caribbean, in Tanzania, in Canada and London; and Rodney's reputation as a scholar-activist of the 1960s and 1970s who had developed a substantial critique of Jamaican, Caribbean and African post-colonial elites was firmly established. In the ten months in 1968 that Walter Rodney had spent in Jamaica, he not only taught on campus but also spoke to groups in the marginalized urban communities of Kingston and in the rural areas. He had an extraordinary ability to speak with and listen to working people and unemployed youth, explaining the significance of Africa to Caribbean history and the importance of the struggles against the racial and social legacies of slavery and colonialism. His articles and speeches embodying these positions were published in the book *Groundings with my Brothers*.

Rodney's intellectual moorings are rooted in a radical black intellectual and activist tradition. C.L.R. James eloquently pointed this out when he wrote,

> Now I, Aimé Césaire, George Padmore, Dr DuBois, and others were faced with a particular challenge. As we grew up and went along, we had to fight the doctrines of the imperialist powers in order to establish some Caribbean foundation or foundations for the underdeveloped peoples. Walter did not have to do that . . . Walter grew up in an atmosphere where for the first time a generation of West Indian intellectuals was able not only to study the revolutionary and creative works that had been created in Europe but also to benefit from and be master of what had been done in the same tradition in direct reference to the Caribbean.[4]

Rodney learnt from James the application of historical materialism so brilliantly applied in James's classic work on the Haitian Revolution, *The Black Jacobins*. However, Rodney's significance went beyond the older generation of Marxists and radical thinkers in two ways. First was his research and understanding of West African history, which gave him a huge intellectual advantage not only over his predecessors but also over all his Marxist contemporaries in the English-speaking Caribbean. He filled in the blanks in our understanding of Africa before the transatlantic trade and plantation slavery. Second, he closely observed the daily activities, lifestyle and cultural expression of Caribbean people and so was attuned to their thinking, practices and life rhythms. Hence, he drew from them in ways that deepened his understanding of their strengths and weaknesses. As such, he was able to assess their capabilities in the struggle for decolonization. Marxism was an intellectual tool; it was the scaffolding for his practical and intellectual labours. His academic research, teaching and activism in the 1960s and 1970s were geared towards decolonization and transformation of the lives of the mass of the population. Decolonization was occurring in an international context shaped by the Cold War between the Soviet Union and the United States. Meanwhile, the Chinese Revolution that had taken place under Mao Tse Tung was still finding its own way towards economic growth. It did so through trial and painful errors committed, especially in the cultural revolution in the 1960s and 1970s.

The coincidence of the Cold War and the movement towards decolonization marked an ideological battleground of ideas about capitalism and socialism. Meanwhile, the United States was waging wars against liberation movements in Vietnam, Angola and Mozambique in Southern Africa and was a bastion of support for the apartheid regime in South Africa. Like the United States, which had built its capitalist economy on the enslavement of Africans, the colonial powers of Britain, France, Holland, Portugal, Denmark and others had also built strong capitalist economies based on slavery and the development of global plantation systems, which contributed significantly to the rapid industrial development of their metropolitan domestic economies. The United States through the Marshall Plan, a massive investment project, enabled Western Europe to rebuild after the Second World War. No such assistance was forthcoming from European powers for their former colonies when political decolonization occurred in the mid to late twentieth century.

TWO

Africa had been subjected to colonial and racially based political systems controlled from metropolitan capitals in Britain, France, Holland, Germany and Belgium and had been assigned a specific role in the global capitalist order as cheap labour and raw material exporters. The partitioning of Africa that occurred in the 1880s had been contested by African resistance, but as with the opposition to the slave trade, superior technology in weaponry made a decisive difference in favour of Europe. Two European wars of 1914–18 and 1939–45, in which several million Africans, African American and Caribbean people fought for democracy in Europe, forced colonials to realize that these doctrines of freedom and democracy were denied them while they were dying for these values in Europe. Nationalist movements developed in Africa and the Caribbean while the struggle by African Americans for civil liberties continued apace. These movements mutually enriched each other. It is out of this ferment, influenced by radical movements in India and China, that leaders emerged in Africa and the Caribbean and gained constitutional power.

These leaders faced enormous challenges for social, cultural and economic development demanded by their populations. Julius Nyerere's Arusha Declaration of 1967 saw Tanzania defining itself as a socialist state, with the intention not only of overhauling the institutions of the state but also initiating a programme of collectives in agriculture designed as ujamaa villages.

President Nyerere defined his mission not only to take on these challenges but also to provide financial and logistical support for liberation movements fighting for freedom in Southern Africa. Tanzania, therefore, hosted liberation movements from Southern Africa, which included the African National Congress (ANC), Front for the Liberation of Mozambique (FRELIMO) and Popular Movement for the Liberation of Angola (MPLA). Radical students and staff were among those who took the lead in developing their response to this initiative. As such, Walter Rodney, during his sojourns in Dar es Salaam 1966–67 and 1969–74, was an active participant in the critical debates around these policy shifts.

His years in Tanzania from 1969 to 1974, Pat Rodney described as the best years in the life of the family. The family was at home in Dar es Salaam, and Pat appreciated the civility of the people she worked with as a public health nurse in the Dar es Salaam City Council. She thus developed her connections with working people, wherever she lived, enabling her to make significant contributions to public health education in the Caribbean and in the United States. Her book, *The Caribbean State – Health Care and Women – An Analysis of Barbados and Grenada* undertook a comparative study of public health systems during 1979–83, the years of the revolution in Grenada. She later directed the Master of Public Health Program, Morehouse School of Medicine, Atlanta, Georgia.

She had identified with the Tanzanian people and was frequently mistaken as a native. "Tanzania was our first 'family home', and it was a magnet for friends and colleagues from Tanzania, and other African countries, North America and Europe, with whom we met for food, music, conversation and discussions about the socio-political changes in East Africa and throughout the region."[5] The children were loved, and this was also Walter's most creative period in which he expanded his reach in African history from West Africa to East and Southern Africa.

Rodney saw African nationalism as a progressive and historically necessary force and sought to develop a dialogue between nationalist theories and Marxism. His speculative essay, "Tanzanian Ujamaa and Scientific Socialism", is a good example of this dialogue.[6] He argued that the modes of production that Marx developed for Europe were not a universal sequence, and conditions in Asia needed to be analysed to discover new directions for socialism. So that while Marx speculates about the Asiatic mode of production, Rodney proposed there could be an African mode of production. He advanced that: "The word 'Ujamaa' had been popularized in two contexts: first, as referring to the extended family of African communalism; and second, regarding the creation of agricultural collectives known as Ujamaa villages. The relation between the two is that the Ujamaa villages seek to recapture the principles of joint production, egalitarian distribution and the universal obligation to work which were found within African communalism."[7]

Rodney differentiates Nyerere's Ujamaa from the African socialism promoted by Leopold Senghor and Tom Mboya, arguing that "When 'African Socialism' was in vogue early in the 1960s, it comprised a variety of interpretations ranging from a wish to see a socialist society in Africa to a desire to maintain the status quo of neo-colonialism."[8] Nyerere's approach was more critical of capitalism and certainly of imperialism. But Nyerere was not a Marxist. In advocating Ujamaa as a route to socialism, Rodney wrote, "The most important requirements were: first, that the 'traditional' forms should exist in real life and have some social vitality; and second, that international conditions should be favorable owing to a socialist breakthrough in some part of the world. For Africa, the fulfilment or non-fulfilment of these conditions needs to be examined."[9]

Rodney's search for a different way to socialism faced the formidable strength of the international capitalist system, as neither China nor the Soviet Union was economically strong enough to provide the support required by so many post-colonial countries in Africa and Asia. The idea of disengagement from the Western capitalist system discussed in the work of the Egyptian economist, Samir Amin, was not a viable option because the international options were too weak. This political option would only result in political authoritarian rule in the face of Western economic, political and military policies. Moreover, the internal struggle within the ruling party in Tanzania caused the country to go in a different direction from Rodney's hopes; and the allies he had in the leadership, such as Abdulrahman Babu, who served as minister of planning, were later imprisoned by Nyerere. But Rodney's point concerns thinking about Marxism in conditions of Africa's historical development and rejecting the imposition of Europe's developmental stages on Africa. To some extent, he was seeking a non-capitalist path to socialism. Rodney quotes Amilcar Cabral to support his position.

> Amilcar Cabral put his finger on these points and explains lucidly that the possibility of such a jump in the historical process arises mainly, in the economic field, from the power of the means available to man at the time for dominating nature, and, in the political field, from the new event which has radically changed the face of the world and the development of history, the creation of socialist states.[10]

These are big historical perspectives that assume a global change in the world order coupled with technological changes that make it possible for leaps in development to occur. I refer to Rodney's essay as speculative, as he was not advancing a policy position but theorizing about the possible futures of the African revolution. In these reasonings, his standpoint is that "Masses of people have to enter into an epistemology and a methodology different from those to which they have been accustomed."[11] Colonial and racist epistemologies had to be destroyed. In examining the leadership of independence struggles, Rodney saw the emergence of a petty-bourgeoisie that had no wealth of its own, had no history of production, was educated in the colonial paradigms and worked in teaching, a limited range of professions, theology – both Moslem and Christian, and public administration and who rose to power in the nationalist movement. When the change-over of power occurred, the state became the source of enrichment through access to public resources and contracts. This stratum functioned through political parties or through the military when civilian power was overthrown. Rodney describes the petty-bourgeoisie as "a local social stratum that lives in a privileged manner in colonial or post-colonial society".[12] Amilcar Cabral in his famous lecture "The Weapon of Theory" spoke of the petty-bourgeoisie in the following way:

> By virtue of its objective and subjective position (higher standard of living than that of the masses, more frequent humiliation, higher grade of education and political culture, etc.), it is the stratum that soonest becomes aware of the need to rid itself of foreign domination. This historical responsibility is assumed by the sector of the petty bourgeoisie that, in the colonial context, one might call revolutionary, while the other sectors retain the characteristic hesitation of this class or ally themselves to the colonialist to defend, albeit illusorily, their social position.[13]

Following Cabral's lead, Rodney saw this stratum as one with various possibilities – from support for revolutionary change to lukewarm and hostile attitudes. There is therefore always a struggle within this stratum over the direction of society in the struggle against colonialism and after the constitutional handover of authority. Drawing on Cabral's notion of class suicide, the hope was that in a revolutionary struggle for a new society these aspirations could be suppressed or frustrated. While this idea of class suicide could function in the bush during armed struggle where the rules of revolutionary combat and self-discipline could be enforced, sometimes brutally, against comrades who fell afoul of political and moral standards, they could not be sustained over the long haul of economic development. In other words, class evolution and development could not be restrained solely by politics, laws and ethics.

Rodney's educational work to develop a radical consciousness was informed by the fact that the students he taught in Dar es Salaam in classes and study groups would become the political, administrative and business leaders in Africa. They would presumably lean towards post-colonial transformation and not shift into new class positions of privilege and use social status as leverage for enrichment in collaboration with Western imperialism. Issa Shivji recalls Rodney's activism and the Sunday ideological classes he led during a period of "intense debates and struggles and intellectual ferment" concerning Tanzania's development. His activism was not confined to the campus as he went out to work in Ujamaa villages in the rural areas.[14] John Saul describes the left at the University of Dar es Salaam as "[comprising] the most active members of the Tanganyika African National Union (TANU) Youth League and the University Students' African Revolutionary Front (USARF)".[15] The chairman of USARF was Yoweri Museveni, later president of Uganda. Rodney wrote for *Cheche*, the student revolutionary journal. But neither USARF nor *Cheche* lasted because of opposition in the Nyerere government to their left-wing position. A paper Rodney wrote and presented to the Second Seminar of East and Central Africa Youth in December 1969, "The Ideology of the African Revolution", got a stern response in an editorial published in *The Nationalist*, the organ of TANU, Tanganyika African National Union, the ruling party, for its advocacy of revolutionary violence. The editorial warned, "Both Tanzanians and non-Tanzanians in this country must accept two things. The subversion of our constitution, and use of Tanzanian facilities to attack other Africans states, are both equally unacceptable here. Surrounding them with revolutionary jargon, and the use of words like 'imperialist', 'neo-colonialists', and 'capitalists', does not alter their unacceptability. Those who insist upon indulging in such practices will have to accept the consequences of their indulgence."[16] These threatening words were directed at Walter Rodney and, according to Shivji, were penned by Mwalimu Nyerere.

In his response, Rodney accepted the idea of non-interference, arguing that "it is not meaningful to call for or work for revolution in countries where one does not live, work or struggle. That is the prerogative of the people involved, who have the necessary social experience of the particular countries".[17] When Shivji suggested to Rodney that he should apply for Tanzanian citizenship, he paraphrased Rodney's response, "Comrade, I don't know the idiom of the people here. I cannot immerse in the people and struggle with them. I have to go back to the people with whom I can communicate and be part of."[18]

The years in Tanzania were very productive, as he was immersed in a dynamic developmental discussion over agrarian reforms. Rodney was an excellent teacher and started a development studies programme at the University of Dar es Salaam. In 1972, he published his best-known work, *How Europe Underdeveloped Africa*. This work brings together historical scholarship and development theory to argue that the transatlantic slave trade and Western capitalist slavery did severe damage to Africa in depriving Africa of millions of its young people during the sixteenth to nineteenth centuries. It was also devastatingly critical of the impact of colonialism on retarding the development of the continent.

How Europe Underdeveloped Africa begins by defining the concepts of development, underdevelopment and the law of uneven development. He establishes the dialectical relationship between development and underdevelopment in the trade relations between Africa and Europe after the fifteenth century and points to uneven economic and technological development between Europe and Africa. But uneven development also relates to internal economic development on the continent, which had different modes of production – from hunter-gatherers to farmers to manufacturing using metals and developing textile production. Rodney's focus on uneven development is a term that encompasses inequality and is especially relevant in today's era of global uneven development. The theoretical rigour of *How Europe Underdeveloped Africa*, which establishes the interconnectivity between the rise of capitalism in Europe and Africa's assignment as a pool for enslaved labour service and resources, is what holds together this historical work covering more than five hundred years of human history on the continent of Africa and in the Americas and Europe.

In the period of political independence, the question of

underdevelopment, poverty, inequality, low levels of literacy, small numbers of engineers, health personnel, entrepreneurs, weak infrastructural development and governmental institutions came to the fore in national and international policy discussions. The state, according to Kwame Nkrumah, would be an instrument of transformation in Ghana and a vehicle for Pan-Africanism. President Julius Nyerere also saw the state in this way. Comparisons were naturally being made with more economically developed economies, many of which had derived substantial wealth through the transatlantic slave trade, colonialism, and the exploitation of their own working classes. Western economies led by the United States in the post–Second World War years structured the financial and trading systems in ways that benefited them and disadvantaged newly independent states. The Soviet Union was not economically strong enough in its history to be an economic competitor to the West or to provide viable options to newly independent countries though it made considerable efforts to give military and educational support to national liberation struggles in Asia and Africa during the years of the Cold War as part of the global geo-political struggle. In this context, there was a struggle between power elites in Washington and Moscow to influence the leaders of newly independent states in Asia, Africa and the Caribbean over choices between capitalism and socialism and the role of the state and private capital. The term 'Cold War' suggests sharp ideological conflict but not military confrontation among the big powers. There were no wars in Europe or the United States, but NATO countries and United States fought wars and overthrew governments in Asia,

Africa, Latin America and the Caribbean in which millions died. Hence, the era of the Cold War must be seen as a time of "Hot Wars" for the rest of the world. The Soviet Union and China were also involved in the opposing sides of these conflicts.

In the era of Hot Wars, developing states were being encouraged in different directions, some towards state-led socialist development and others towards capitalist development. The two major players on the global stage, the Soviet Union and the United States, were the ideological trendsetters, but Tanzania chose non-alignment and followed its own path. Here, the challenge faced by newly independent governments was broadly speaking how to transform the economy and the choice of what policies were necessary to develop the wide range of capabilities in the public and private sectors to meet the urgent needs of the population for health care, education, security, housing and the essentials of living.

In *How Europe Underdeveloped Africa*, Rodney decided not to start with that mid-twentieth century political dichotomy but focused on Africa's human development before the transatlantic trade and colonialism as a lead-up to the period of Western imperial domination. He illustrates the universality of development, starting from the initial stages of human society. At the basis of the process of development is the labour of humans – the first basic requisite of all human life and the development of tools which facilitate man's productive activity in each system of production relations. The dominant activity in Africa prior to the intervention of the Europeans in the fifteenth century was agriculture; and he emphasizes advanced methods such as terracing, crop rotation, manuring, mixed farming, and regulated swamp farming. Furthermore, iron tools such as the axe and hoe had evolved. But he suggests that the persistence of communalism in Africa was itself a regressive factor in the development of production since it checked the emergence of a class system. The class system, as it evolved from communal forms, saw a contradictory development. On the one hand, the expansion of productive forces using more complex tools that raised output. On the other hand, it led to the appropriation of the surplus by the owners of the means of production. These were ideas that came out of the economic theories of Adam Smith and Karl Marx. Some nations had also been making progress in manufacturing, for example, the rise of tailoring guilds in Timbuktu, of the glass and leather industries in northern Nigeria; the extensive development of trade and monetary relations in North Africa, Ethiopia and Congo.[19]

Rodney's exploration of African history and development was crucial, as the average Caribbean citizen was as ignorant of African history, and still is, as Africans are of Caribbean history, and still are. While considerable new research and publications have developed since Rodney's time in the 1960s and 1970s, this body of work has not had the required impact on educational systems in Africa and the Diaspora. For instance, while there is much written about resistance to slavery in the African Diaspora, particularly the Haitian Revolution, which brought an end to slavery, insufficient attention has been paid to resistance to the slave trade on the continent. Rodney's thesis on the Upper Guinea Coast documents both African resistance and collaboration as the transatlantic trade became a central profit-making industry for Western European capitalism. West and Central Africa had many small competing states, which made it possible for European states to play one state against another. And those larger states that resisted, over time, were subordinated by the military and economic strength of the Europeans. Rodney wrote,

> In the Congo, the slave trade did not get under way without grave doubts and opposition from Africans who had established contact with the Europeans. The King of the state of Kongo clearly defined the nature of his expectations from Europe. He asked for masons, priests, clerks, physicians, and the like; but instead he was overwhelmed by slave ships sent by his Catholic brothers in Portugal, and a vicious trade was opened up by exploiting contradictions within the loosely structured Kongo kingdom.[20]

With Angola, Queen Nzinga's resistance to the Portuguese in Angola was followed by her subordination evidenced in the change of her name to Dona Ana de Sousa, which symbolized a shift in cultural identity that legitimized the control of Portugal over Angola.[21]

Africans fought alien political rule, yet some Africans opposed the abolition of slavery because it constituted a significant part of their economic activities. Rodney concluded that "For most European capitalist states, the enslavement of Africans had served its purpose by the middle of the nineteenth century, but for those Africans who dealt in captives the abrupt termination of the trade at any given point was a crisis of the greatest magnitude."[22]

In his essay, "Labour as a Conceptual Framework for Pan-African Studies" Rodney writes of Europe's Africa contact in the fifteenth century, "West Africa in the fifteenth century boasted skills in brass casting and plastic arts, advanced techniques in canoe-building and river travel, and notions of agriculture relevant to tropical forests, savannahs, and swamps. Europe, on the other hand, had superiority to some extent in arms technology and to an overwhelming extent in shipbuilding, navigation, administration, and accounting."[23] What then were the skills that Africans brought with them in the centuries of the transatlantic trade?

> Several of the people of the Senegambia who were victims of the slave trade were experienced as pastoralists and familiar with open-pit mining of gold and iron ore. Crops such as cotton, indigo and rice were produced in the American colonies and the Caribbean by Africans who were already growing those same crops in their own societies. It could hardly be a mere coincidence that rice production was successfully launched in the Brazilian state of Maranhão in the mid-eighteenth century just at the moment when African labour was being brought in from the traditional rice-farming sector of Upper Guinea.[24]

So African skills contributed significantly to the plantation capitalist economies of the Americas.

In his essay "Historical Roots of African Underdevelopment", he points out the internationalization of trade that developed in the fifteenth century in which Europe systematically repositioned Africa as suppliers of human beings. "They owned and directed the great majority of the world's ocean-going vessels, and they controlled the financing of trade between four continents. Africans had little clue as to the tri-continental linkages between Africa, Europe, and the Americas."[25] Rodney makes clear the items traded by Africans were limited. They included, "things such as civet perfume, ambergris, indigo, monkeys and feathers; but, of course, those were mere curiosities. The economically significant commodities were few and were chosen by Europeans in accordance with European needs".[26]

In the fifteenth and sixteenth centuries, Europe surged past Africa because of the rapid development of navigational and military technology. This launch led it to the global trade in Africans that was the foundation of the plantation economies of the Americas and the Caribbean in sugar, cotton and other exports. Rodney shows how the slave trade boosted the international financial system so much so that David and Alexander Barclay, leading eighteenth-century slave traders, later used the loot to set up Barclays Bank. The same applies to Lloyds Bank and the insurance houses of Britain, which were all major investors in the slave trade. During the late 1800s, the colonial period worsened economic and social underdevelopment in Africa. The continent was dragooned into international trade, mainly controlled by Europe. This trade focused on extracting raw materials, often using slave labour. For example, in the early 1900s, the Belgians exploited the Congo through such practices. From the time of the slave trade to the era of independence, various African states, nations and leaders played a role in enabling this exploitative process. Writing of the years of political independence, Rodney contended sarcastically, "Any diagnosis of underdevelopment in Africa will reveal not just low per capita income and protein deficiencies, but also the gentlemen who dance in Abidjan, Accra, and Kinshasa when music is played in Paris, London, and New York."[27]

In thinking about global trade, Rodney argued for conditional support for socialist countries trading with Africa, "Africa is also diversifying its trade by dealing with socialist countries, and if that trade proves disadvantageous to the African economy, then the developed socialist countries will also have joined the ranks of the exploiters of Africa."[28]

Rodney also voiced several ripostes to the racialized assumptions underlying British historiography on Africa and the Caribbean. His essay, "The British Colonialist School of African Historiography and the Question of African Independence", is a classic Walter Rodney demolition of several colonial arguments. Among these are that Britain prepared its colonies for independence. Rodney dismantled the positions of a British journalist, John Hatch, at a Sunday morning seminar at the University of the West Indies in 1968. This same polemic is repeated in a later publication where he posited that "Governors like Arden-Clarke (Gold Coast), Renison (Kenya), Turnbull (Tanganyika) and Hugh Foot (Jamaica) presided over the dissolution of the British Empire with unquestioned skill; but it is certainly questionable whether they led or guided towards independence, as distinct from compromising with a reality that had outrun expectations."[29] Rodney emphasized instead the significance of the mass political movements led by Kwame Nkumah in the Gold Coast, Jomo Kenyatta in Kenya, Julius Nyerere in Tanganyika and the nationalist movement in Jamaica which gave rise to Alexander Bustamante and Norman Manley in forcing political concessions from the British.

But he also argued that the impact of the trade in Africans and colonialism was also cultural and psychological. He wrote that "the people of Africa and other parts of the colonized world have gone through a cultural and psychological crisis and have accepted, at least partially, the European version of things. That means that the African himself has doubts about his capacity to transform and develop his natural environment".[30] He therefore advocated for educational transformation that would engage these negative legacies. He initiates his challenge to this brainwashing by identifying indigenous systems of education in Africa whose growth was impeded. He points to the knowledge that a Fulani has of some seventy to eighty varieties of cows and knowledge of plants in the forest and their uses. He was pointing to what we now refer to as Indigenous Knowledge Systems. He confirmed this approach by quoting from J.E. Casely Hayford, an African nationalist from the Gold Coast, who wrote, "Before even the British came into relations with our people, we were a developed people, having our own institutions, having our own ideas of government."[31] Part of this development was the extent of environmental knowledge. Rodney emphasized that by the "fifteenth century, Africans everywhere had arrived at a considerable understanding of the total ecology – of the soils, climate, animals, plants, and their multiple relationships. The practical application of this lay in the need to trap animals, to build houses, to make utensils, to find medicines, and to devise systems of agriculture."[32]

In the same year of the appearance of *How Europe Underdeveloped Africa*, his doctoral thesis turned monograph, *A History of the Upper Guinea Coast 1545–1800* was published by Oxford University Press. In 1975, he had two chapters on "The Guinea Coast" and "Africa in Europe and the Americas" in the *Cambridge History of Africa.* The latter essay was a pioneering study of the African Diaspora. For its part, *How Europe Underdeveloped Africa,* provided a framework for our understanding of global history and development in the age of decolonization. Development theory needed to be translated into politics, and it is in the political arena during the Black Power era that the protests by the Jamaican people against the ban imposed on him by the government of Prime Minister Hugh Shearer made him a household name in the island and brought him international attention. His years at Dar es Salaam had been his most productive. According to Pat Rodney, it was also the best time for family togetherness, as they enjoyed economic security and stability before the political turbulence following their departure from Tanzania.

THREE

The day 16 October 1968 started out as a student protest by undergraduates outraged at the government's decision to prevent the re-entry of Rodney into Jamaica after he had attended a Black Writers' conference in Montreal. Led by the UWI Guild President Ralph Gonsalves and dressed in their scarlet gowns, the student protesters who marched to the Jamaican Parliament were joined by hundreds of young people who had their own grievances, some of which were fuelled by the teargassing and beating of demonstrators by the police. Therein lay the making of an uprising in Kingston which triggered a political crisis for Prime Minister Hugh Shearer, leader of the Jamaica Labour Party, the political organization which had led Jamaica to independence in 1962. Shearer continued banning and censorship policies that had been implemented by the British and by Norman Manley, leader of the opposition People's National Party. When Rodney later visited Jamaica in 1978 to attend the founding congress of the Workers' Party of Jamaica, he had to secure a waiver. Neither the Jamaica Labour Party nor the People's National Party lifted the ban on Walter Rodney.

Three hundred and seven years of British slavery and colonialism marked all aspects of life in Jamaica. During Rodney's sojourn in 1968, the principal groups that articulated claims for reparative justice were the Garveyites, Ras Tafari and radicalized sections of the middle and working classes. Many educated Jamaicans saw Britain in a positive light, cultivated pseudo-British accents and went on "home leave" to London if they were civil servants. This obsession with being British was not only among the middle classes but also among poor people and peasants who spoke well of British royalty. Empire Day, 24 May, the date of Queen Victoria's birthday, was celebrated in schools throughout the British colonized Caribbean. Schoolchildren observed the rituals of Empire Day and pledged allegiance to the British sovereign. As a result, Africa was seen as an uncivilized and barbaric continent; and there was considerable self-hate or what Garvey had referred to as internal prejudices held by black people. One question Rodney could answer in his talks was: Who were we before the transatlantic slave trade and plantation slavery? In a population where the majority were black and clearly derived from the continent of Africa, few people could answer this question. Rodney's clear-cut brief essays in *The Groundings with My Brothers* were revelations, as many young people still saw their nationality forged in slavery as their true beginning. This view was sustained by the state through the educational curricula from early childhood to university, as the history of Africa was absent from the educational system. On the other hand, the racial question was deeply embedded in the Jamaican social structure and had shaped its social and economic relations, especially its system of plantation ownership, its large agro-proletariat on the sugar and banana estates, its peasantry which predominated on hillside lands and produced crops for the internal market, the emergent brown and black middle classes, and the ethnic minorities who dominated the commercial and financial fields.

But before Rodney, a racial awakening had been underway in Jamaica led primarily by Rastafari in the decade of the 1960s.[33] Rodney had observed in one of his talks in 1968 that: "The racial question is out in the open in spite of all the efforts to maintain the taboos surrounding it. The Rastafari brethren have been joined on this question by large numbers of other black people – many of them influenced by the struggle and example of black brothers in the United States – while culturally, there is a deepening interest in things African."[34] The racial question was the Achilles heel of Jamaican social and economic structure sustained by its political arrangements.

Rodney's talks on "African History and Culture" were crucially effective in affirming awareness of the island's African heritage. The essays in *The Groundings with My Brothers* are steeped in Garveyism, and Rodney frequently quoted from Garvey's writings on African history in introducing his series. While he lectured on the history of the large states associated with African civilizations in Egypt, Ethiopia and Western Sudan, he pointed out the many small states and some of the traditional values around which African communities had been built:

Among the principles of African culture, the following are to be noted: hospitality, respect (especially to elders), importance of the woman (especially in cases of inheritance), humane treatment of lawbreakers, spiritual reflection, common use of land, constant employment of music (especially drums) and bright colours. Some of these principles are found in many different human societies, but very few are encouraged in the present white capitalist world. Even in Africa itself, European slave trading and colonization have destroyed many aspects of African culture. But culture is not a dead thing, nor does it always remain the same. It belongs to living people and is therefore always developing. If we, the blacks in the West, accept ourselves as African, we can make a contribution to the development of African culture, helping to free it from European imperialism.[35]

This message resonated because the communities of Rastafari had identified long ago as African and had initiated new spiritual values in their communities, some of which coincided with those outlined in Rodney's talk. He stressed the Garveyite message of self-confidence: "What we need is confidence in ourselves, so that as blacks and Africans we can be conscious, united, independent and creative. A knowledge of African achievement in art, education, religion, politics, agriculture and the mining of metals can help us gain the necessary confidence which has been removed by slavery and colonialism."[36]

Rodney also observed that the Rastafari were emphatic in making the call for reparative justice, saying that the twenty million pounds paid by the British government to the planters should have been paid to the enslaved Africans. The dominant narrative in Jamaica was that the British monarch had been responsible for emancipation from slavery because of the campaigns of William Wilberforce and others. But the role of the Haitian Revolution and the Sam Sharpe Christmas rebellion of 1831–32 were not mentioned as key factors in abolition.

Rodney gave two talks on Black Power. The first was published as "Black Power, A Basic Understanding". Here, he references Garvey as one of the "first advocates of Black Power and is still today the greatest spokesman ever to have been produced by the movement of black consciousness".[37] In this talk, he spoke about the movement in the United States that had been effective in raising consciousness globally about the struggle against anti-black racism. A critical question raised in the movement had to do with violence and Rodney was clear-cut in stating that "Violence aimed at the recovery of human dignity and at equality cannot be judged by the same yardstick as violence aimed at maintenance of discrimination and oppression."[38]

Rodney's understanding of the continuing impact of racial slavery and Indian indentureship meant he saw the relations between Africans and Indians as critical in the struggle against imperialism. For this reason, his interpretation of Black Power embraced these subordinated groups and others such as the indigenous populations of the Caribbean. Rodney concluded that,

> it is obvious that the West Indian situation is complicated by factors such as the variety of racial types and racial mixtures, and by the process of class formation. We have, therefore, to note not simply what the white world says but also how individuals

> perceive each other. Nevertheless, we can talk of the mass of the West Indian population as being black – either African or Indian. There seems to have been some doubts on the last point and some fear that Black Power is aimed against the Indian.[39]

This layered understanding of race and ethnicity in the Caribbean was characteristic of Rodney's grasp of the complexity of the social and racial structure and his refusal to see things in black and white. How people perceive themselves and each other becomes an important variable in consciousness and has a considerable impact on dissonance, prejudice and conflict in multi-ethnic societies. So in his definition of Black Power, he highlights the history of racial slavery and indentureship, but he also recognizes the conflicts based on ethnicity and colour that divide oppressed groups. Rodney's affirmation of the solidarity between oppressed Indians and Africans was a hallmark of the political outreach of the youthful leadership of the National Joint Action Committee (NJAC) during their marches and demonstrations in the 1970 Black Power uprising in Trinidad and Tobago.

Turning to the Jamaican situation Rodney asserted, "The present government knows that Jamaica is a black man's country. That is why Garvey has been made a national hero, for they are trying to deceive black people into thinking that the government is with them. The government of Jamaica recognizes black power – it is afraid of the potential wrath of Jamaica's black and largely African population."[40] The massive protests on 16 October 1968, demonstrated the prophetic nature of Rodney's statement. Rodney rejected the notion of "black supremacy" articulated in some Rastafari circles, arguing "all other groups in the society . . . can have the basic right of all individuals but no privileges to exploit Africans as has been the pattern during slavery and ever since".[41]

The unravelling of centuries-old racial privileges and the achievement of a democratic order had certainly not been part of the constitution-making process. Black faces as head of state representing the British sovereign and prime ministers who looked like most of the population failed to change the racial order. The racial order was, however, disturbed by the Black Power movement and Rastafari activism with support from other social groups throughout the Caribbean in the 1960s and 1970s.

Rodney had appealed to the intelligentsia to link with the interests of the mass of the population:

> Black Power, within the university and without, must aim at overcoming white cultural imperialism. This act is brought out in virtually any serious sociological study of the region – the brainwashing process has been so stupendous that it has convinced so many black men of their inferiority . . . The adult black in our West Indian society is fully conditioned to thinking white, because that is the training we are given from childhood. The little black girl plays with a white doll, identifying with it as she combs its flaxen hair . . . 'Good hair' means European hair, 'good nose' means a straight nose, 'good complexion' means a light complexion . . . and . . . black is the incarnation of ugliness.[42]

Too often Marxist-Leninists in the Caribbean dismissed followers of the Black Power Movement as cultural nationalists who lacked a class perspective. An example of this was Cheddi Jagan's 1972 article on "Cultural Nationalism" collected in his pamphlet, *A West Indian State: Pro-Imperialist or Anti-Imperialist*; this position was characteristic of all Marxist-Leninist groups which were organized in the region. The political line was that race and culture were superstructural factors and racism would be eradicated when the working class came to power and capitalism was overthrown. Revolutionary thinkers like Amilcar Cabral and Walter Rodney understood the importance and relative independence of culture from economic relations and the enormous significance of race as one of the global structures of capitalist exploitation and political oppression. Rodney, who participated in the debates around Black Power and Marxism in the 1970s, contended that:

> our history imposes upon a black Marxist the necessity to operate almost exclusively, certainly essentially, within the black community. Now I know that will be likely to sound heretical to many Marxists because they will say, but surely your constituency is the working class and you should therefore transcend, rather than be prisoner of, the racial divisions within the class, because these racial divisions are essentially divisions at the subjective level of consciousness. This is how the traditional argument will go.[43]

But Rodney pointed out that race is not a matter of subjectivity, and it is not eliminated merely by educating the white worker, as white racial privilege is embedded in the structures of government, the cultural and social system, as well as the economic order of racial capitalism. Racial privilege is therefore a central component of global capitalism arising from the transatlantic trade in Africans and plantation slavery, which shaped American and European capitalism. This order exists also in Latin America and the Caribbean. Rodney's research, writing and activism in different locations where black people lived confirmed the strong race, class and gender oppression of these regions; and Jamaica mirrored all these features.

Jamaica had gained independence in 1962 and Prime Minister Alexander Bustamante, leader of the Jamaica Labour Party, had reputedly stated, "We are with the West." Not surprisingly, he was clear on the continuity of Jamaica's international relations with Britain and the United States. As such, he was hostile to the Soviet Union and China and those who spoke out in support of socialism. Later adherents of Black Power were deemed subversive, and the Rastafari movement was seen as a threat to national security. Prime Minister Bustamante continued the colonial repression against Rastafari, as evidenced in the beatings and imprisonment of Rastafarians after the 1963 Coral Gardens incident:

> At the root of the incident was the long-standing demand for land by the rural poor and the resort to squatting which many had taken up as well as the intense discrimination against Rastafarians in all areas of social life . . . Rudolph Franklin had been shot and sentenced to a prison term in 1962 after a land dispute in the Rose Hall area, near Montego Bay, a main tourist area. The attack by Rastafarians on a gas station resulted in eight people being killed – among them two policemen and three Rastafarians. The incident created panic in the country and led to the arrest of 150 Rastafarians in four parishes.[44]

However, the aftermath of Coral Gardens saw the cutting of locks [matted hair] and beatings and imprisonment of Rastafari throughout the island. The police force became the symbol of "Babylon", not only for Rastafari but also for the grass-roots youth population. The government had vilified Rastafarians and their ideas of Jamaica's African heritage, and the police had licence to arbitrarily intimidate them by cutting off their locks and beating them up when they were arrested. But there was growing resistance to these abuses among young people who were influenced by the growing tide of racial consciousness in the 1960s, expressed in the Black Power and Civil Rights movement.

It was, therefore, not surprising that at independence, legislation was passed to ban black publications from the United States. On 18 July 1968, under The Undesirable Publications Law, the following were banned: "All publications of which Stokely Carmichael is the author or co-author; All Publications of which Malcolm X called Malcolm Little is the author; All Publications of which Elijah Muhammed is the author."[45]

The year 1968 was a turbulent year, with the assassination of Martin Luther King, which led to protests in one hundred American cities, the emergence of the Black Power and Black Panther organizations, the Black Power salute by John Carlos and Tommie Smith at the Mexico Olympics, mass protests against the United States war in Vietnam, protests in Prague, Czechoslovakia against Soviet troops and the anti-capitalist politics of the student movement in France and Germany.

Walter Rodney returned to Jamaica in January 1968 from the University of Dar es Salaam. His return to UWI was eagerly expected, as he was the first UWI graduate to earn a PhD in African history, and he would have anchored the teaching and research in this area. He knew Jamaica well, as during his undergraduate student years from 1960 to 1963, he had travelled around the island and had been engaged as an undergraduate in the campaign for West Indian federation. He had already become a target of the police Special Branch because of his visits as a student to Cuba and the Soviet Union and his links with Southern African liberation movements in Tanzania.

The Jamaican population he returned to was experiencing racial awareness as black self-confidence was on the rise in the mid-1960s. The 1960s in Jamaica had witnessed the Reynold Henry guerrilla movement of 1960, the activities of Millard Johnson's Garveyite People's Political Party; Bustamante's repression of Rastafari in the 1963 Coral Gardens incident; the return from England of Garvey's body to Jamaica for reburial in 1964; the protest against a Chinese shopkeeper's abuse of a black woman in 1965; the visit of Emperor Haile Selassie to Jamaica in 1966, which had a huge impact on the Rastafari community and the four-year-old nation; the national state of emergency of 1966–67, which saw increased repression and surveillance of progressives. Two important movements had helped to shape this consciousness – activists influenced by Garvey's ideas and the militant Rastafari movement, especially the activism of Leonard Howell from the 1930 to the 1960s. The British government and Alexander Bustamante, founder of the Jamaica Labour Party, had raided Howell's headquarters in Pinnacle, near the old capital of Spanish Town and not far from Kingston, subjecting him to police harassment and eventually locking him up. A younger generation of activists, this time with dreadlocks, had emerged and had produced two emblematic figures, Mortimo Planno in West Kingston and

Ras Negus in Dunkirk in Central Kingston. Planno was an influential mentor to singers such as Bob Marley and in July 1968 had put on a concert in Kingston with several artistes who were to gain fame in the 1970s, thus pioneering the development of reggae.

Walter and Pat Rodney had a particular impact on the community of students at the university, as they were a black couple who constituted a particular role model for young people. The students had previously encountered black academics who had studied in the United Kingdom and returned with white wives or had married light-skinned women. That had been the case with generations of lawyers, doctors, engineers, dentists and academics. To see a black lecturer with a PhD married to a young woman with an afro who was pursuing higher education, who were comfortable with each other and socialized with all irrespective of class, said more to students than brilliant talks. The Rodneys' presentation of themselves spoke volumes about their integrity and commitment. Some female students and young women copied Pat Rodney's Afro-style, and their love and care as young parents were inspirational.

So, when on 15 October the students gathered at a meeting, the main argument that brought out their sympathy and determination to protest was the rupture of this family, especially because Pat was pregnant with the Rodneys' second child, Kanini. In addition, there was a Black Power group on the Mona campus, and there were publications to which Rodney contributed. Among these were *Blackman Speaks*, edited by Jerry Small; *Scope*, the UWI Guild newspaper; and *Bongo-Man* (1968–70), which this present author published.

Rodney's work also appeared in the *Social Scientist* (journal of the Faculty of Social Sciences). Jerry Small, Garth White and Peter Phillips were activists from the middle class who had adopted Rastafari beliefs and were living in urban communities of the poor. This trend in the 1960s would gather steam in the 1970s. Such people were also involved with the sound-systems of the time, which promoted popular music and "rude-boy" culture. Rude-boy culture was developed by borderline low-paid working-class youths on construction sites, by informal traders, hustlers and the unemployed who daily were living hand-to-mouth. Recruits from this stratum entered the political parties as enforcers during electoral campaigns or formed gangs that developed their own enterprises and harrassed communities and businesses. They became targets for elimination by the police. They too were part of the audiences receptive to Rodney's reasoning within urban communities of the poor.

That link between the educated middle strata, the urban poor, especially the rude boys and Rastafari, could result in a flammable situation and that was what exploded on 16 October, when the grievances ordinary people had against the state, the violence inflicted by the police and unemployment erupted in an unexpected mass protest. Many of those in the protests did not even know Rodney. But at the youthful age of twenty-six, he had the intellectual and physical energy to pursue his academic work and was as active on-campus as he was off campus. He was the treasurer of the African Studies Association of the West Indies (ASAWI) on the UWI Mona campus and connected to the Afro-Jamaican associations off campus. He was, in fact, part of a vibrant academic group on the Jamaica campus of the University of the West Indies. Among the decolonial lecturers at UWI's Jamaica campus were Prof. Elsa Goveia, a brilliant Guyanese historian who was the first UWI Professor in history and a female at that; Lucille Mair, the warden of the all-female hall of residence, who was an activist scholar on gender in her work on Caribbean history and later Jamaica's representative at the United Nations. There was the Barbadian doctor Kenneth Standard, who developed community health training programmes and outreach, especially in the adjoining community of August Town; Sylvia Wynter who was taking on epistemic questions about the Caribbean and was developing ideas about how the literature of the Caribbean across multiple languages could be reconfigured and taught. Through the *Jamaica Journal*, published by the Institute of Jamaica, she was writing thought-provoking essays on the island's cultural identity.[46] There was Ken Post, a Marxist political scientist who taught African Politics and Modern Political Thought. The New World Group initiated by Lloyd Best in British Guiana in the early 1960s was an attempt to develop a Caribbean-wide intellectual community that would spearhead the discussion about transformation of the region. An outstanding economist was George Beckford, one academic who marched with the students in 1968, and whose work on the plantation systems in Latin America and the Caribbean led him to write the classic text, *Persistent Poverty – Underdevelopment in Plantation Economies of the Third World* that was published in 1972, the same year as *How Europe Underdeveloped Africa*. Then there was the distinguished Caribbean poet, historian and cultural critic Edward Kamau Brathwaite.

But the main new marker on the cultural landscape was the music that was emerging in the communities of West and East Kingston in vocals and instrumentals, which introduced new genres of popular music that were inextricably tied to global freedom struggles. One of the popular tunes in 1968 was "Everything crash" by a group called The Ethiopians. The song was emblematic of the protests.

Walter Rodney's "Message to Afro-Jamaican Associations" was published in *Bongo-Man* in early 1969. In his statement to a conference about Africa-oriented associations, Rodney made several important observations. On Marcus Garvey, he wrote, "They brought Garvey's bones but not his philosophy." This was a sharp critique as Garvey's body had been repatriated from London to Kingston in 1964, and the government had announced that he would be made Jamaica's first National Hero. However, there was no attempt to address his philosophy, and some regarded this movement as a symbolic manipulation of Garvey's legacy, which ignored the philosophical substance of his work that was so important in debunking the myths of racial inferiority. Garvey's widow, Amy Jacques Garvey, and his son, Marcus Garvey Jr, who was completing his degree in physics and mathematics at the University of the West Indies in 1968, were outspoken critics of the regime's decision to ban black literature and Walter Rodney. The seventy-two-year-old Amy Jacques Garvey, whom I visited weekly, was in correspondence with a wide range of Black Power personalities and Pan-Africanists, and hence she was frequently denied access to share her views on radio. She stood at her gateway on 12 Mona Road, giving vocal support to the students as they marched by. Of her, Rodney wrote,

Jamaicans are extremely fortunate in still having amongst them, [the] wife of Marcus Garvey, and a Black revolutionary fighter in her own right. She must be protected, and the best use made of her services. It will be interesting to see whether the government will be brazen enough to move openly against the Garvey family and the Garveyite philosophy when it is fully propagated. Then, even the blind will see.[47]

In his message, Rodney wrote about the Rev. Claudius Henry, R.B. (repairer of the breach). Claudius Henry's son, Ronald Henry, had been involved in an armed struggle against the Jamaican state in 1960 and was killed by a joint force of some five hundred police, as well as Jamaican and British soldiers. Rodney wrote:

The government has charged me with the crime of consorting with Rev. Henry, which means that he is a criminal. It is unnecessary here to refute those wild charges. One must understand that such accusations come from a set of frightened men alarmed by a massive demonstration of black solidarity. Rev. Henry's name is mentioned here specifically in connection with the question of economic re-awakening, for although his organization is basically religious, it carries out a policy of economic co-operation and self-reliance among black people. At Kemp's Hill, in the middle of a most depressed area which is the Prime Minister's constituency . . . .[48]

Rodney's presence in the prime minister's rural Clarendon constituency is the key to understanding why Shearer was so intent on expelling Walter Rodney from Jamaica. One Saturday morning, I accompanied Walter to a service held by the Rev. Claudius Henry. Walter was not asked to speak, but he listened and observed the awakening that was occurring in rural Jamaica as well as in the poor urban communities.

The ban on Walter Rodney initiated a radical turn in Caribbean political life as protests occurred in the region as groups emerged, questioning political independence. Frantz Fanon's *Wretched of the Earth* was a key text in political education among young people and the conclusion many drew was that with constitutional independence truly little had changed in the lives of the people. White domination was intact, preferential access by white and light-skinned people to financial credit for business, management and promotion in the private sector were retained. Hotels and clubs discriminated against black people and social and mainstream religious institutions had similar barriers that restricted black access. It was not long before a sustained fightback against racial barriers and the capitalist plantation system ensued throughout the Caribbean under the banner of Black Power. The 1968 uprising had repercussions throughout the region and the diaspora and created a political climate that favoured radical change.

FOUR

From the Rodney uprising of 1968 in Kingston through to the Grenada revolution of 1979 a young generation of political activists made this period the most radical moment since the regional labour protests of the 1930s in British Honduras, St Kitts, St Vincent, St Lucia, Trinidad, Barbados, the Bahamas, Jamaica, Antigua and British Guiana.[49] Thirty years later, the Black Power movement took hold in all these territories.[50] Among the hallmarks of these years were the 1970 Black Power Revolution in Trinidad and Tobago, which saw the largest and most sustained demonstrations occurring between February and April 1970. Prime Minister Eric Williams deployed the military against the Black Power demonstrators, but Lieutenants Raffique Shah and Reginald "Rex" Lasalle refused to attack the demonstrations; and their act of solidarity resulted in a mutiny in the army that could have led to the overthrow of the regime. In response to the Black Power movement, Williams combined reforms and repression. Reforms led to state ownership in the finance and petroleum industries and an increase in social expenditure on health and education. Repression took the form of the jailing of Black Power leaders and mutinous army men. It also led to the brutal suppression of the National Union of Freedom Fighters, active between 1972 and 1974, that had started a guerrilla struggle on the assumption that the protest marches were inadequate so that an assault on the state was necessary. The army killed their leaders, and supporters were targeted and detained.

By 1972, Jamaica, Guyana, Barbados, and Trinidad and Tobago had established diplomatic relations with Cuba, the Soviet Union and China, thus defying the United States. Moreover, some Caribbean states went further, with Jamaica and Barbados facilitating the refuelling of Cuban planes flying to Angola with troops. "Between November 1975 and April 1976 36,000 Cuban soldiers poured into Angola."[51] This act was the single most important factor in the decision of Henry Kissinger to use the CIA and economic pressure to destabilize the Michael Manley government in Jamaica. In 1979, there was the overthrow of Eric Gairy's regime in Grenada, led by the New Jewel Movement of Maurice Bishop and Bernard Coard, which attracted the support of hundreds of young people in and outside the region who volunteered to work to transform that country. Also in 1979, the Sandinistas came to power in Nicaragua.[52] In 1980, Desi Bouterse seized power in neighbouring multi-ethnic Suriname.[53]

Of significance for Guyana and Walter Rodney was the example of the United Labour Front in Trinidad and Tobago founded in 1976, which brought together the Oilfield Workers Trade Union led by the dynamic George Weekes; the All Trinidad Sugar Estates and Factory Workers Trade Union organized by Basdeo Panday; the Transport and Industrial Workers Union led by Joe Young; and the Trinidad Islandwide Cane Farmers Association led by Raffique Shah.[54]

Throughout the decade of the 1970s, the unions were struggling to remove Eric Williams from power and were doing so on a multiracial platform. This was an example of what was possible, but it would be more difficult in Guyana where the unions were not only rigidly rooted in Indian and African ethnic constituencies and linked to the two main political parties but bitter memories of the racial riots in 1964 in British Guiana haunted the political landscape. Those riots were the worst expression of ethnic violence seen in the region. Cheddi Jagan in his book, *The West on Trial – The Fight for Guyana's Freedom*, said violence resulted from the strike action of sugar workers represented by the Guyana Agricultural Workers Union, which was opposed by the Trades Union Council, the government-backed union. The sugar workers were predominantly Indian, while the government was dominated by Africans. "The toll for the 1964 disturbances was heavy. About 2668 families involving approximately 15000 persons were forced to move their houses and settle in communities of their own ethnic group . . . Over 1400 homes were destroyed by fire. A total of 176 people were killed and 920 injured. Damage to property was estimated at about $4.3 million and the number of displaced persons who became unemployed reached 1342."[55]

Walter Rodney was jolted by these developments, and while researching for his doctoral dissertation in London, he was preoccupied with the ethnic question in his homeland. He presented a paper entitled, "Notes towards a Popular History of Guyana" to a Guyana Symposium held in London, 23–24 October 1965. That lecture anticipates his posthumously published *A History of the Guyanese Working People, 1881–1905*. In 1965, Rodney concluded,

> To castigate loyalty to ethnic group as the cause of Guyana's present mess is superficial – just as superficial as blaming imperialism in toto for the increase in racial confrontation. Simple and definitive explanations must give [way] to a more sober analysis of the complexities of the development of the Guyanese mass movement – of the relationship between racial consciousness and racial prejudice, between economic competition and racial conflict, between communal identification and class objectives.[56]

In his essay "Masses in Action" published in the Guyana Independence issue of the *New World* journal in 1966, Rodney embarked on a historical discussion of the contradictions between the African and Indian groups. He wrote, "What occurred in the period after 1955 was that communal awareness was, for several reasons, turned inwards to exacerbate racial contradictions among the Guyanese workers and peasants. I say 'exacerbate' because racial conflict in Guyana was an inevitable concomitant of the fact that indentured labour (East Indian, Chinese and Portuguese) was conceived to break the back of Negro opposition to the planter class."[57] Rodney also pointed out that "between 1900 and 1928, the situation was entirely different. Then, it was the awareness among both Indians and Negroes of the peculiar disadvantages under which their own race laboured that precipitated an attack on colonial society."[58] Here, Rodney is exploring the historical moments in which class interest and advocacy by both groups emerged, focusing on their common economic and social problems. This was a theme that was crucial to his political work in the formation of the political movement in Guyana in the 1970s. This movement was the Working People's Alliance (WPA), which brought together a young and hopeful generation of Indo- and Afro-Guyanese political activists.

Rodney's critique of the West Indian petit bourgeoisie in power identified the features of political life which needed changing, and a platform emerged from his assessment. He argued that "constitutional decolonization almost invariably concluded with a political arrangement from which the masses are excluded and one which provides the political basis for neo-colonialism".[59] He identified the features of neocolonialism under petty-bourgeois leadership, by which he meant the middle strata drawn from professional groups. These features were the concentration of power in the hands of the petty bourgeoisie; destruction of popular political expression and participation; the manipulation of race and other divisions amongst the people; the institutionalization of corruption; the extension of political repression and victimization; the vulgarisation of "national culture" as a tool for class rule; and the deliberate distortion of revolutionary concepts.[60]

Shiva Naipaul, Vidia Naipaul's brother, contests Janet Jagan's opinion that "Guyana 'is not in reality a stratified, racially divided nation'. Well, what was Guyana if it were not a racially divided nation?"[61] A strict class analysis could not make headway in Guyana's demographic where racial identification dominated not only political consciousness but affective behaviour in friendship, marriage, religion, residential and community formation. Rodney grappled with the complex implications of these relations for personal freedom and democracy. While in Tanzania, Rodney had missed active engagement with the groups in the Caribbean that had been in transition from Black Power to Marxism-Leninism, but he had kept abreast of developments and was keen on immersion in the political and intellectual life of Guyana and the region.

So in 1974, he resigned from the University of Dar es Salaam and headed back to Guyana to an uncertain future. But neither Walter nor Pat could secure employment in Guyana because of their opposition to Forbes Burnham's authoritarianism. Rodney even applied to teach at one of the secondary schools:

> My application to join the staff was first dispatched from Tanzania in 1972 at a time when I had already taken the decision to return to Guyana. No vacancy existed. I re-applied recently when the post of professor of history was advertised. The second application was acknowledged, but no further official communication was received from the University until a letter dated 23rd August which simply advised me that I had not been selected . . . It is now well-known that my appointment was approved through the regular academic channels and that it was disallowed for supposedly political reasons. In this connection, it is necessary for me to draw attention to the fact that I have been absent . . . and I have never actively participated in the national political life.[62]

But President Forbes Burnham saw in the young scholar-activist a political opponent whom he preferred to have either outside the country or on his side. This was the beginning of the duel between the Machiavellian Forbes Burnham and the intrepid Walter Rodney. While there is truth in this perception, it overlooks the thousands of especially young people who were actively engaged in the struggle for a democratic order. For them, Walter had become the leader. In Burnham's mind, Rodney's multiracial activism undermined Afro-Guyanese political solidarity and strengthened the Indo-Guyanese People's Progressive Party (PPP).

The PPP was affiliated with the international communist movement and was politically aligned with the Communist Party of the Soviet Union (CPSU) in the Cold War. At the 25th anniversary party conference of the PPP in 1975, Jagan noted that the ruling party was advocating Marxism-Leninism.[63] This meant that the main political parties in Guyana were not only politically left-of-centre but had relations with the CPSU. In 1975, American-owned bauxite mines were nationalized; and in the following year, British-owned sugar estates and refineries were taken over by the state. The Leonid Brezhnev–led CPSU helped to influence Jagan's attitude to the ruling PNC and to shape its critical support policy, Burnham's anti-democratic policies within Guyana notwithstanding.

This decision would have had inputs from Fidel Castro and Cuba's Communist Party, given their knowledge of Latin America and the Caribbean. Although the CPSU had ties especially with communist parties in Argentina, Brazil and Chile, it was still in the phase of learning the history and politics of Latin America and the Caribbean and adjusting to the wave of leftism and guerrilla warfare in the 1960s, influenced by Fidel Castro and Che Guevara. The United

States was the hegemon and had long favoured Burnham, notwithstanding their disagreements with his nationalization policy, his support for African liberation movements and his electoral manipulation. He could count on US support while pursuing a foreign policy of developing relations with Cuba, China and the Soviet Union. He also provided military training and gave guns to Maurice Bishop's New Jewel Movement in Grenada to help overthrow Prime Minister Eric Gairy's repressive regime in March 1979.

Jagan succinctly described the new policy at a party congress in 1975, "Our political line should be changed from non-cooperation and civil resistance to critical support."[64] Jagan's position of "critical support" reflected policy shifts in the CPSU that encouraged support for progressive regimes in the developing world. Burnham's PNC was seen as a radical party by the CPSU and the Communist Party of Cuba, and it was a member of Socialist International, which brought together social-democratic and labour parties.

The PPP for a while gave the governing party "critical support" for reforms that it had enacted but opposed abuses of power. In a 1975 letter to Harry Drayton, Guyanese scientist and Marxist, Rodney wrote: "Jagan's critical support speech met with some rather insulting responses that he should prove himself to be genuine, and the only measurable result so far has been a tendency to allow the PPP to feature occasionally in the news."[65]

The WPA itself was divided on its attitude to the PPP, according to Rodney:

FOUR

> The WPA found it impossible to come to a unanimous conclusion on the implications of the actions of the PPP. One of our constituent groups took a hard line that the PPP was responding to foreign dictates and were selling out the working class. Another was more hopeful that the new policy might arrest certain neo-fascist trends and perhaps force changes within the PNC and PPP. Of course, our own work continues as before, although there is the possibility that we might be isolated as ultra-leftists.[66]

This tag of ultra-leftism was typical of the political language of time and was targeted at those who did not follow one orthodoxy of Marxism emerging from Moscow or Peking or Latin American parties and groups. In Guyana, the label had poignancy, given the existence of three competing left-wing parties, with the WPA being a new organization appealing across ethnicity to young activists.

Meanwhile, Rodney did not buy into Moscow's or Jagan's reassessment of Burnham but exposed it. But in the Guyanese political spectrum, the WPA was the junior political party having been formed in 1979. It brought together ASCRIA (African Society for Cultural Relations with Independent Africa), led by Eusi Kwayana, the Indian Political Revolutionary Association, the Working People's Vanguard Party, the group at the University of Guyana around the *Ratoon* newspaper and Movement Against Oppression.[67] The Ratoon group had developed on the University of Guyana campus in the wake of Rodney's ban in Jamaica in 1968. The Ratoon group comprised the University of Guyana biologist Josh Ramsammy, economists Compton Bourne, Maurice Odle and Clive Thomas and Omowale (plant physiologist).[68] The Movement Against Oppression (MAO) was organized in the working-class community of Tiger Bay. Ramsammy, Clive Thomas, Andaiye, Eusi Kwayana and Brian Rodway were among the movers.

The first issue of *Ratoon*, 14 October 1969, followed the publication of the *Abeng* in Jamaica in early 1969. The publication of *Abeng* was followed by a host of cyclostyled publications and leaflets published through the Caribbean in these years. In Trinidad, there were *Tapia*, *Moko*, smaller grass-roots publications such as *Pivot* and *East Dry River Speaks*. *Black Star* and *Caribbean Contact* – published by the Caribbean Conference of Churches headquartered in Barbados – *Outlet* (Antigua), and *YULIMO* (St Vincent) were other new left-of-centre publications.

The WPA had decided on a structure of joint leadership in keeping with the consultative process it had developed in conducting its affairs. The group included Roopnarine, Rodney, Kwayana and Andaiye. Andaiye pointed out that Rodney "was fully involved in the discussion of the 1979 party program but he was not fully involved in the debate on the party's constitution . . . Rodney's preference was for mass agitation and Roopnarine spearheaded the work on the constitution and party-building efforts . . ."[69] Rodney was not a proponent of self-proclaimed vanguard organizations such as the Workers' Party of Jamaica, which tried to adapt to Jamaican conditions Lenin's ideas on party organization. Rupert Roopnarine argues that Rodney "was fully in support of the cadre formation: highly motivated cadres, disciplined, with a rigorous division of labour, need to know principles of revolutionary work, round-the-clock availability and other forms of sacrifice unavailable in less centralist organizations. This was of course a perquisite in the self-defence security units."[70] Roopnarine was, however, closer in his organizational thinking to the Workers Party of Jamaica than was Walter Rodney.

Andaiye provides a sense of the WPA leadership with her characteristic sardonic wit: "From 1978 to when Walter was killed, I was party coordinator (a job that often included unblocking blocked toilets, by hand) and party editor for *Dayclean* and all other party publications. I also had another job – to be available to listen to personal problems in my house at any hour of the night; Walter coined the name Mrs Packer (Personal Affairs Committee) for me."[71] But the WPA leaders were movement activists and were not inclined to representational politics. "I don't personally know anybody in the WPA who wanted to run the state, who saw themselves as the [prime minister] . . . ."[72]

In the growing consciousness signalled by the left-of-centre publications in the region, Rodney travelled to Trinidad in 1978 where he addressed an Oilfield Workers Trade Union (OWTU) rally on 19 June, observed as Labour Day, and spoke to a crowd of fifteen thousand people. Rodney received support from the OWTU for strikes that were then occurring in Guyana. The OWTU, led by the legendary labour leader George Weekes, had financially supported working-class struggles in Guyana, Grenada and Dominica.

The year 1979 was a year of political explosions captured well in Sparrow's calypso, "Wanted Dead or Alive" in which he listed several tyrants who had fallen. Among them Idi Amin in

Uganda, the Shah of Iran, Vorster's resignation in South Africa, Eric Gairy in Grenada, the fall of Patrick John in Dominica, Somoza in Nicaragua, Park Chung Yee in South Korea, among others. The political work done in 1978 enabled the WPA to grow its support, which peaked in 1979. On 27 July 1979, when the PNC's secretariat was burned down, the blame was placed on the WPA; and the police arrested and charged Rodney, Roopnarine and Omowale with arson. There was a tremendous outpouring of support at their trial. This was when the political momentum shifted towards the WPA. Prior to 1979, the WPA had with limited financial and material resources been building support from young working people and sectors of the middle class and civil servants disillusioned with the politics of Jagan's PPP, but especially against Burnham's authoritarian leadership of the country. The WPA attempted to change the political culture of ethnically based parties by offering a multiracial political organization and programme. Taking on political culture was a strategic goal that was extremely difficult because of the ethnic orientation of the population and the political fact that the principal two parties stood to benefit from the unquestioned support of their ethnic bases. According to Andaiye, the WPA became increasingly organized as it moved from a loose grouping towards party formation in 1979. In this period of civil rebellion, the WPA was holding public meetings throughout Guyana, organizing bauxite workers and holding political education classes.

The record of Burnham's conduct in government demonstrated the correctness of Rodney's oppositional stance since Burnham was constructing a constitutional dictatorship.

It did not take long for people to realize the realism of Rodney's position of critical exposure. For instance, in 1974, Burnham had declared the paramountcy of the party over the state, which meant that state organs such as police, army and civil service were subject to party control. The 1973 election had given Burnham two-thirds of the National Assembly, but he wanted to change the electoral system to bring it more under the control of the ruling party. In 1978, the PPP, WPA, the People's Democratic Movement and the Liberator Party, trade unions, professional and religious groups voiced their opposition to changes in the constitution that would give Burnham's PNC control of the electoral system. Among the issues involved were the "conduct of overseas registration and voting; the organization of registration at home; the conduct of the poll at home; the custody of the ballot boxes after a poll; the subordination of the nominally independent Elections Commission; freedom of speech; freedom of assembly; and the aggravation of ethnic tensions".[73] The idea was to remove the need for a referendum to change the entrenched clauses of the constitution and make it possible for the government with its two-thirds majority in Parliament to change the constitution. Burnham won the referendum, but the Opposition accused him of electoral fraud and overstating the turnout.

While the international press hardly focused on Guyana, the spotlight was shone on the interior of the country when there was a tragedy in November 1978 involving the collective suicide-murder ritual of over nine hundred Americans. Rodney responded to this event, arguing that:

what occurred there was precisely an act of complicity through neglect on the part of both the US and the Guyanese Governments. The US Government had admitted in its reports that it had done far less than it should have done for US citizens who were at Jonestown and some type of intervention on behalf of those citizens might well have avoided the holocaust. The US Government had admitted this. The Guyanese Government had admitted nothing of the kind. The Guyanese government has treated the whole situation as if it were an everyday affair, as though 914 people die in the bush in Guyana every day.[74]

Rodney focused his criticism on Burnham and his links with the People's Temple, an African American group, from which thugs were drawn to beat up those who attended the public meetings of opposition groups, especially the WPA.

African Americans were drawn to Burnham's party because of its Pan-Africanist stance, and he had extended an invitation to them to come and settle in Guyana. Some did. Burnham's black nationalism was in full play, and his African American supporters, among whom was the prominent writer Julian Mayfield, were militant in supporting their sponsor.

Political violence was one tool that Forbes Burnham deployed against his opponents. As early as 4 October 1971, Josh Ramsammy, a biologist and activist at the University of Guyana, was shot and injured in an assassination attempt. Then in 1979–80, years when the WPA was on the offensive, Walter Rodney, Rupert Roopnarine and Omowale, WPA leaders, were arrested for burning down the Ministry of National Development. Father Bernard Darke, Jesuit priest and photographer for the *Catholic Standard*, was stabbed fatally in the back by thugs of the House of Israel on 14 July 1979, while taking pictures of a demonstration in support of the WPA leaders. Michael James, the editor of the *Catholic Standard*, and his wife were beaten up. Later, two WPA activists were killed: Ohene Koama was killed on 18 November 1979 and on 25 February 1980 Edward Dublin, who had been Rodney's bodyguard, was shot and killed by the police. Walter himself had to run for his life from a public meeting in Georgetown on 22 August 1979, where thousands had gathered. Eusi Kwayana wrote: "Suddenly, a group of uniformed policemen, including Rabbi Washington's men dressed in police uniform and carrying no regulation numbers, attacked the meeting which they claimed was illegal. It was a total assault with batons on the crowd of peaceful citizens by a crowd of well-armed policemen of the Tactical Service Unit (Riot Squad)."[75] At a congress of the ruling PNC, Burnham sarcastically commented on Rodney's athletic "prowess as an athlete and promised to send him to the Olympics".[76]

Given the power of the United States in the region, Rodney occasionally requested audience with the US Embassy in Georgetown. The embassy reported that on 5 December 1979 he assured the Americans that the WPA posed no threat to the United States; but that given the violence being directed against the Opposition, there was no alternative to their taking defensive measures against the thuggery. Rodney also requested that in the event of his murder the embassy would arrange resident alien status for his wife and children. And on 18 January 1980, Rodney, in his capacity as leader of the WPA and Roopnarine as deputy leader, presented the embassy with the WPA's domestic and foreign policy programme. Rodney stressed that "unlike the PPP's Moscow orientation, the WPA and its leaders were not beholden to any foreign power and did not seek such affiliation".[77] However, in the assessment of the embassy officials, the WPA's socialist economic goals were akin to Soviet-style communism.

For his part, however, Rodney's attitude to Burnham's socialism was caustic. He branded it pseudo-socialism, arguing that the PNC incorporated:

> a large proportion of the most reactionary and right-wing elements in the country – groups that used to be in the United Force, groups that used to oppose even the nationalist struggle back in the 1950s. That is not to say that any given individual is incapable of transformation. But we are talking not just of one individual, but of a large number who are clearly representatives of a class which has given no indication, public or private, of any transformation in their world view, their lifestyle or their social objectives. They are encrusted within the party and the government; they represent the party at the highest level inside and outside the country. Overnight they have been given new slogans to shout, and it does amaze me how these slogans don't stick in their throats. It is not a matter of a small deflection here and there; the fellows actually have to turn their sentences around in exactly the opposite direction.[78]

Yet, although preoccupied with activism, Rodney was missing his work as a historian. While working in the archives at the University of Hamburg in 1978, he wrote:

> I have been given an office and I am trying to settle into a work routine. The university is huge and, like others of its type, one of

its greatest resources is its library. In fact, libraries are scattered all around the campus, and the Germans clearly have a serious pre-occupation with documentation. If one had the time, one could sit here indefinitely and write numerous treatises. I sometimes feel a little nostalgic at no longer being an integral part of this world of books, but perhaps if we can achieve something there will be no need to express reservations.[79]

Always productive, Rodney's five lectures at Hamburg were published posthumously in 1984 as *A Tribute to Walter Rodney – One Hundred Years of Development in Africa – Lectures given at the University of Hamburg in summer 1978*. Ambivalence about being politicians could not however be sustained in the face of growing support during the period of civil rebellion of strikes and mass protests in 1979. Walter Rodney, Rupert Roopnarine and Andaiye assumed leadership roles, but there was no doubt of Walter's national prominence as a political leader.

One of his allies was Eusi Kwayana, who exerted a potent moral force he had developed as a schoolteacher in his African free village of Buxton.[80] But he was also an experienced politician who had been a founding member of the PPP in the 1940s, the PNC in the 1950s and the WPA in the 1970s. He was of the older generation, self-disciplined, a vegetarian and somewhat of an ascetic personality. Kwayana's knowledge of Guyana's history and the traditions of struggle in the free villages made his contribution to worker education special. He had been a close associate of two of Guyana's most brilliant sons, the poet Martin Carter and the novelist Wilson Harris. Apart from Kwayana, the WPA boasted a formidable cast of speakers. Among them were Joshua Ramsammy, Tacuma Ogunseye,

Kathy Wills, C.Y. Thomas, Eusi Kwayana, Bonita Harris, Rupert Roopnarine and Walter Rodney. Rodney however was the most compelling speaker whose argumentation was backed up by mastery of contemporary data and a capacity to communicate complex ideas to small study groups and large audiences with great clarity, drawing on his solidly rooted knowledge of African and Caribbean history and political economy.

The 1979 Grenadian, Nicaraguan and Suriname revolutions signalled a radicalization of the region, so the United States was on the alert. There was optimism in Guyana among the opposition forces as well. The 1979 movement of resistance and the "Burnham must go" campaign occurred when Burnham was supplying arms to the New Jewel Movement in their effort to overthrow the Eric Gairy dictatorship in Grenada. But Burnham was at the same time plotting to remove Walter from the scene. The political atmosphere was fraught with anxiety and fear of what Burnham could do to the opposition. It is in this climate that Walter showed his strength and willingness to lead in public meetings and in study groups in private homes. In a letter to Harry Drayton, he was enthusiastic about two Marxist study groups he had founded. One was at Linden, the bauxite mining town, and was:

> purely working class and was at the request of some very advanced workers who have already done a great deal of reading . . . The one at my home is more diluted with respect to class elements, but the whole society can and will benefit from more scientific insights. Besides, as the consequence of deliberate efforts in that direction, the group includes four sisters – their absence having been noteworthy in previous efforts.[81]

Study groups were organized throughout the Caribbean region in the 1970s, familiarizing themselves with radical literature and discussing the local and international situation with a focus on political mobilization. Bauxite workers had organized themselves in the Organization of the Working People. Walter Rodney and C.Y. Thomas taught them classes in political economy and labour economics. Other WPA leaders, such as Eusi Kwayana, also gave talks.

In 1979, the WPA and the PPP assessed Guyana had a revolutionary situation. Cheddi Jagan pointed to the fall of Caribbean governments led by Patrick John in Dominica, Eric Gairy in Grenada and John Compton in St Lucia. More importantly was the outrage of the Guyanese population at the trial of WPA leaders, the murder of Father Darke and the strikes in August by four unions.

Not long before he was murdered, Walter Rodney took a daring trip to Zimbabwe where he had been invited to participate in the independence celebration. Burnham thought Rodney was in Georgetown pending another hearing for the arson trial. So Rodney's trip was a high-risk and complex operation. Roopnarine, co-leader of the WPA, had been one of the key persons organizing Rodney's trip that took him from Georgetown to the Courantyne River then on to Suriname. Roopnarine's graphic description of this risky journey known only to a handful of WPA leadership and Pat Rodney is telling:

> We had, first of all, to get him from Georgetown to the Courantyne [River] . . . we had to go overland. We used about three cars to get him as far as Rosignol. At Rosignol, instead of taking the ferry that we knew would be under surveillance, we

used a small fishing boat and got across to New Amsterdam. From there we had to then go all the way up to the Courantyne, switching cars several times again until we got him to Crabwood Creek. From Crabwood Creek, we took a small fishing boat, in the dead of night, to Nickerie.

On arrival in Suriname, Roopnarine wrote:

the Sergeants' revolt in Suriname had happened. Bouterse and a number of leaders of the Surinamese Revolution were close to us, in the sense that they seemed to be a genuine anti-imperialist revolution. They had a very strong multi-racial outlook . . . they had sent an emissary to Georgetown who had actually spoken with me and Walter . . . when Walter got to Nickerie it was up to the Surinamese authorities to move him. They were able to facilitate that . . . They gave him an entry stamp, and from everything we know from the Zimbabwean episode, Burnham was in a state of shock to find Walter there.[82]

However, Walter's purpose in going to Zimbabwe was not to shock Burnham who was also an honoured guest. According to Roopnarine, it was to get assistance for the struggle. However, no details are provided regarding the help requested, but judging from the mention of logistical difficulties, this help is likely to have included weapons for defence against the increased use of violence by the state. Roopnarine explained that the WPA was at the time "attempting to equip ourselves, essentially ready ourselves, and ready the masses for an insurrectionary attack on the state".[83] President Robert Mugabe's offer to Walter for him to head an Institute in Harare was anti-climactic since leaving Guyana for an academic position would have meant abandoning the fight to remove

Burnham. The paradox was that Burnham had Pan-African credentials with Mugabe and other leaders in Southern Africa, so Rodney's was a difficult request, and it is not surprising that the response was negative. Rodney returned from Zimbabwe somewhat despondent for two reasons. First, his requests for assistance were unsuccessful and second, there was an ebb in the tide of the mass movement that had in 1979 reached the level of a civil rebellion. Walter wrote to friends in Hamburg, Germany, a month before his assassination, pointing out that:

> Since November [1979], there has been a lull in public street activity. As far as the WPA is concerned, this resulted from 3 factors: the seizure of some of our cars and public address equipment by the police, the destruction of other pieces by PNC thugs, the burning of one of our vehicles by the same elements, etc. Secondly, from a decision to put more of our energies into the work of party building, and into bilateral negotiations with party and non-party groupings on the question of a Government of National Unity. And thirdly, from our unwillingness to allow the state to consume our time and energy in this period in the endless round of court appearances that were resulting, and would continue to result, from our confrontations with the police at every picket, demonstration or 'illegal' public meeting.[84]

The principal actor in reversing the movement in the region was the United States government. The United States was quick to respond to the radical turn in the Caribbean in the late 1960s and 1970s, fearing especially the influence of Cuba. The United States was also deeply involved in economic pressure through the IMF, in subversion, in supplying gangs with weapons in Jamaica and in the terrorist bombing of a Cubana plane off the coast of Barbados in 1976, which killed all seventy-six people on board. Henry Kissinger saw the airlifts of Cuban soldiers, planes and weapons facilitated by the governments of Michael Manley, prime minister of Jamaica, and Prime Minister Errol Barrow of Barbados as hostile. From 1976 to 1980, Michael Manley became a target; and the CIA launched covert action supplying weapons to opposition gangs linked to the Jamaica Labour Party, economically pressuring the Manley regime through the withholding of loans and a propaganda campaign through the main national newspaper, the *Daily Gleaner*. Several hundred people succumbed to political violence in the run-up to the 1980 general election, which removed Michael Manley from power. The region was under severe assault and although the Grenada Revolution of 1979 offered some hope of a revival of the region's progressive movement, the policies of the United States and Britain not only crushed the movement for social and economic transformation but also introduced a neoliberal agenda that shaped public policy for the following four decades. This involved the sharp reduction in the role of the state in the economy, trade and financial liberalization, and reduction in expenditure on health and education.

By 1980, the period of civil rebellion of the previous year was over; and discussions towards a government of national unity were on the agenda. This meant talks with the Cheddi and Janet Jagan's People's Progressive Party that was Indian-based and had consistently campaigned for fair elections. It is at the point of the ebb in the tide in favour of the WPA and its talks with the PPP that Burnham struck.

On 13 June 1980, Walter, in the company of his younger

brother Donald, were handed what they thought was a 'walkie-talkie'; but it turned out to be a bomb which blasted Walter to death and injured Donald. The bomb had been delivered by Gregory Smith, a former member of the Guyana Defence Force.

When Forbes Burnham appeared on television to comment on Walter's death, he was in a triumphal mood, telling the lie that Rodney had blown himself up while trying to bomb the prison. It took thirty-six years for a commission of enquiry investigating the murder to free Walter's brother Donald Rodney from the charge of complicity in Walter's death and to establish beyond a doubt that his death was an act of the Forbes Burnham state.[85] Walter Rodney's assassination at age thirty-eight was emblematic of the methods being employed to destroy the progressive movement. Throughout the region, the casualties by death and attrition signalled the end of an important period of hope for regional transformation.

But Rodney's political and intellectual legacy lives on. His *History of the Guyanese Working People, 1881–1905* was published posthumously in 1981. As Rupert Roopnarine points out, Rodney wrote this book "fighting as he wrote, and writing as he fought".[86] While he had been researching and thinking about this topic from the 1960s, its gestation and writing was influenced by the intense political labours of the late 1970s. This work embodies his philosophy on the creative role of ordinary people in the making of history and introduces the contribution of African slaves "to the humanization of the Guyanese coastal environment" in creating an elaborate system of canals to provide drainage, irrigation, and transportation in a remarkable transfer of Dutch technology to a coastal landscape that was below sea level.[87] This was to have been the first volume on the Guyanese working people in the twentieth century. In 1982, *A History of the Guyanese Working People, 1881–1905* won the American Historical Association's Albert J. Beveridge prize; and in 1983, the Association of Caribbean Historians also gave a posthumous award. Another published volume was his edited work *Guyanese Sugar Plantations in the Late Nineteenth Century.* Rodney's reputation as a historian of the Caribbean has therefore been duly recognized. Rodney harnessed history in the service of African and Caribbean decolonization to give his readers a sense of their creative capacity to build post-colonial societies. The Barbadian novelist George Lamming in his foreword to *A History of the Guyanese Working People, 1881–1905* described Rodney's approach to history as "a way of ordering knowledge which could become an active part of the consciousness of an uncertified mass of ordinary people, and which could be used by all as an instrument of social change. He taught from that assumption. He wrote out of that conviction".[88]

On 23 June 1980, thousands of Guyanese and other Caribbean citizens, including this author, "walked over a distance of twelve miles behind the murdered body of this young historian".[89]

Thanks to the work of the Walter Rodney Foundation – led by Dr Pat Rodney, Shaka, Kanini and Asha his children – a new generation is discovering Walter Rodney's prolific work, marked by a profound sense of revolutionary commitment to the working people across racial and ethnic boundaries and to the liberation of Africa. The publications by Verso in

2018, 2019 and 2022 of his work give new life to his legacy. Furthermore, Leo Zeilig's biography positions Rodney in the aftermath of the murder of George Floyd in 2021 and the rise of the Black Lives Matter movement. In addition, the way in which his writings flow into the reparation movement is clear in Hilary Beckles's *How Europe Underdeveloped the Caribbean: A Reparation Response to Europe's Legacy of Plunder and Poverty.* This later book confirms the centrality of Rodney's work to twenty-first century global struggles. There is now a Walter Rodney chair at the University of Guyana, so hopefully with proper funding, his work will become better known in the land of his birth, childhood and death as new generations discover the genius of his thinking and pathfinding endeavours.

NOTES

1. Colin A. Palmer, *Cheddi Jagan and the Politics of Power: British Guiana's Struggle for Independence* (Chapel Hill: The University of North Carolina Press, 2010), chapter 1.

2. Walter Rodney, *Walter Rodney Speaks: The Making of an African Intellectual* (New Jersey: Africa World Press, 1990), 8.

3. Alissa Trotz, ed. *The Point is to Change the World: Selected Writings of Andaiye* (London: Pluto Press, 2020), 7.

4. Rupert Lewis, *Walter Rodney's Intellectual and Political Thought* (Kingston and Detroit: The Press University of the West Indies and Wayne State University Press, 1988), 36–37.

5. Walter Rodney, *The Groundings with My Brothers* (London: Verso, 2019), 79.

6. Walter Rodney, *Decolonial Marxism: Essays from the Pan-African Revolution* (London: Verso, 2022), 223–45.

7. Ibid., 223.

8. Ibid., 224.

9. Ibid., 232.

10. Ibid., 235–36.

11. Ibid., 245.

12. Walter Rodney, "Some Implications of the Question of Disengagement from Imperialism," in *Socialism in Tanzania: An*

Interdisciplinary Reader: Policies, vol. 2, edited by Lionel Cliffe and John S. Saul (Dar es Salaam: East Africa Publishing House, 1975).

13. Amilcar Cabral, *Unity and Struggle: Speeches and Writings of Amilcar Cabral*, with an introduction by Basil Davidson and biographical notes by Mario de Andrade (New York: Monthly Review Press, 1979), 135.

14. Issa G. Shivji and Godwin R. Murunga, ed., *Where is Uhuru?: Reflections on the Struggle for Democracy in Africa* (Dar es Salaam: E & D Vision Publishing, 2009), 160, 161.

15. Ibid., 161.

16. John Saul, "Radicalism and the Hill," in *Socialism in Tanzania-an Interdisciplinary Reader: Policies*, vol. 2, edited by Lionel Cliffe and John S. Saul (Dar es Salaam: East Africa Publishing House, 1975), 289.

17. Shivji and Murunga, *Where is Uhuru?*, 163.

18. Ibid.

19. Rupert Lewis, "Walter Rodney's *How Europe Underdeveloped Africa*: A Marxist Approach," *African Studies Association of the West Indies, Bulletin*, no. 6 (1973): 79. For an exposition of *How Europe Underdeveloped Africa* using recent data, see Karim Hirji, *The Enduring Relevance of Walter Rodney's How Europe Underdeveloped Africa* (Quebec: Daraja Press, 2017).

20. Rodney, *Decolonial Marxism*, 97.

21. Ibid., 98.

22. Ibid., 125.

23. Ibid., 77.

24. Ibid., 78.

25. Ibid., 92.

26. Ibid., 94.

27. Walter Rodney, *How Europe Underdeveloped Africa* (London: Verso, 2018), 33.

28. Ibid., 28.

29. Rodney, *Decolonial Marxism*, 177.
30. Rodney, *How Europe Underdeveloped Africa*, 26.
31. Ibid., 35.
32. Ibid., 44.
33. See Rex Nettleford, *Mirror Mirror: Identity, Race and Protest in Jamaica* (Kingston: William Collins and Sangster [Jamaica] Ltd, 1970) for a contemporaneous discussion of the Rastafari and Black Power movements in Jamaica in the 1960s. See also Obika Gray, *Radicalism and Social Change in Jamaica, 1960–1972* (Knoxville: Tennessee University Press, 1991) and Terry Lacey, *Violence and Politics in Jamaica, 1960–1970* (Manchester: Manchester University Press, 1977).
34. Rodney, *The Groundings with My Brothers*, 6.
35. Ibid., 35–36.
36. Ibid., 36.
37. Ibid., 14.
38. Ibid., 16.
39. Ibid., 24.
40. Ibid., 27.
41. Ibid., 26.
42. Ibid., 29.
43. Rodney, *Walter Rodney Speaks*, 102.
44. Lewis, *Walter Rodney's Intellectual and Political Thought*, 90.
45. Ibid., 142, fn. 48.
46. Sylvia Wynter and Demetrius L. Eudell, ed., *We Must Learn to Sit Down Together and Talk about a Little Culture: Decolonising Essays, 1967–1984* (Leeds: Peepal Tree Press, 2022).
47. Walter Rodney, "Message to Afro-Jamaica Associations," *Bongo-Man* (1969): 15–16.
48. Ibid., 16.
49. See O. Nigel Bolland, *On the March: Labour Rebellions in the British Caribbean 1934–1939* (Kingston: Ian Randle Publishers, 1995) for

documentation of the regional labour uprisings in the British Caribbean.

50. See Kate Quinn, ed., *Black Power in the Caribbean* (Gainesville: University of Florida Press, 2014) for the Black Power movement in some Caribbean countries.

51. Piero Gleijeses, *Visions of Freedom: Havana, Washington, Pretoria, and the Struggle for Southern Africa, 1976–1991* (Chapel Hill: The University of North Carolina Press, 2013), 19.

52. See Brian Meeks, *Caribbean Revolutions and Revolutionary Theory: An Assessment of Cuba, Nicaragua and Grenada* (London: The MacMillan Press, 1993).

53. See Rupert Roopnarine, *The Sky's Wild Noise: Selected Essays* (Leeds: Peepal Tree Press, 2012) for discussion of the links between the revolutions in Suriname and Grenada and their impact on the movement in Guyana.

54. See Selwyn Ryan, *Eric Williams: The Myth and the Man* (Kingston: University of the West Indies Press, 2009), 455.

55. Jagan 1972b, 311.

56. Walter Rodney, "Notes Towards a Popular History of Guyana," Guyana Symposium held in London, 23–24 October 1965, 6.

57. Walter, *Decolonial Marxism*, 32.

58. Ibid., 30.

59. Lewis, *Walter Rodney's Intellectual and Political Thought*, 209.

60. Ibid., 10.

61. Shiva Naipaul 1982 , 94.

62. Statement by Rodney, cyclostyled, Georgetown, 18 September 1974.

63. Lewis, *Walter Rodney's Intellectual and Political Thought*, 223.

64. Kempe-Ronald Hope, *Guyana: Politics and Development in An Emergent Socialist State* (Oakville: Mosaic Press, 1985), 59.

65. Lewis, *Walter Rodney's Intellectual and Political Thought*, 215.

66. Ibid.

67. Ibid., 219. See also Quinn, *Black Power in the Caribbean*, 150.
68. See Harold Drayton, *An Accidental Life* (Hertford: Hansib Publications, 2017), 714.
69. See Lewis, *Walter Rodney's Intellectual and Political Thought*, 231.
70. Ibid.
71. Trotz, *The Point is to Change the World*, 50.
72. Ibid.
73. Lewis, *Walter Rodney's Intellectual and Political Thought*, 225–26.
74. Ibid., 227.
75. Eusi Kwayana, *Walter Rodney* (Georgetown: Working People's Alliance, 1988), 15.
76. Ibid.
77. See https://nsarchive.gwu.edu/briefingbook/human-rights/2020-06-13/the-walter-rodney-murder.
78. Lewis, *Walter Rodney's Intellectual and Political Thought*, 223.
79. Rodney in letter to Harry Drayton, 12 April 1978. See Harold Drayton, *An Accidental Life* (Hertford: Hansib Publications, 2017).
80. "Free villages" were formed of ex-enslaved inhabitants who pooled resources to buy up declining plantations in the years following emancipation in 1838.
81. Rodney in letter to Harry Drayton, 23 September 1975. See Drayton, *An Accidental Life*.
82. Clairmont Chung, ed., *Walter Rodney – A Promise of Revolution* (New York: Monthly Review Press, 2012), 109–10.
83. Ibid., 112.
84. Rodney in Lock and Tetzlaff 1984, 133.
85. See Walter Rodney Foundation website: https:\\www.walterrodneyfoundation.org.
86. Trotz, *The Point is to Change the World*, 248.
87. Walter Rodney, *A History of the Guyanese Working People, 1881–1905* (Kingston: Heinemann Educational Books, 1981), 2, 3.
88. Lamming 1981, xvii.
89. Ibid.

BIBLIOGRAPHY

Bolland, O. Nigel. *On the March: Labour Rebellions in the British Caribbean 1934–1939*. Kingston: Ian Randle Publishers, 1995.

Cabral, Amilcar. *Unity and Struggle: Speeches and Writings of Amilcar Cabral*. With an Introduction by Basil Davidson and Biographical Notes by Mario de Andrade. New York: Monthly Review Press, 1979.

Chung, Clairmont, ed. *Walter Rodney – A Promise of Revolution*. New York: Monthly Review Press, 2012.

Drayton, Harold. *An Accidental Life*. Hertford: Hansib Publications, 2017.

Gleijeses, Piero. *Visions of Freedom: Havana, Washington, Pretoria, and the Struggle for Southern Africa, 1976–1991*. Chapel Hill: The University of North Carolina Press, 2013.

Gray, Obika. *Radicalism and Social Change in Jamaica, 1960–1972*. Knoxville: Tennessee University Press, 1991.

Hirji, Karim. *The Enduring Relevance of Walter Rodney's How Europe Underdeveloped Africa*. Quebec: Daraja Press, 2017.

Hope, Kempe-Ronald. *Guyana: Politics and Development in An Emergent Socialist State*. Oakville: Mosaic Press, 1985.

Jagan, Cheddi. *A West Indian State: Pro-Imperialist or Anti-Imperialist*. Georgetown: Sunday Mirror, 1972a.

———. *The West on Trial: The Fight for Guyana's Freedom*. New York: International Publishers, 1972b.

Kwayana, Eusi. *Walter Rodney*. Georgetown: Working People's Alliance, 1988.

Lamming, George. *A History of the Guyanese Working People, 1881–1905*. London: Heinemann Educational Books, 1981.

Lacey, Terry. *Violence and Politics in Jamaica, 1960–1970*. Manchester: Manchester University Press, 1977.

Lewis, Rupert. "Walter Rodney's *How Europe Underdeveloped Africa*: A Marxist Approach." *African Studies Association of the West Indies, Bulletin*, no. 6 (1973): 77–82.

———. *Walter Rodney's Intellectual and Political Thought*. Kingston and Detroit: The Press University of the West Indies and Wayne State University Press, 1988.

Meeks, Brian. *Caribbean Revolutions and Revolutionary Theory: An Assessment of Cuba, Nicaragua and Grenada*. London: The MacMillan Press, 1993.

Naipaul, Shiva. *Journey to Nowhere: A New World Tragedy*. New York: Penguin Books, 1982.

Nettleford, Rex. *Mirror Mirror: Identity, Race and Protest in Jamaica*. Kingston: William Collins and Sangster (Jamaica) Ltd, 1970.

Palmer, Colin A. *Cheddi Jagan and the Politics of Power: British Guiana's Struggle for Independence*. Chapel Hill: The University of North Carolina Press, 2010.

Quinn, Kate, ed. *Black Power in the Caribbean*. Gainesville: University of Florida Press, 2014.

Rodney, Walter. *Decolonial Marxism: Essays from the Pan-African Revolution*. London: Verso, 2022.

———. *The Groundings with My Brothers*. London: Verso, 2019.

———. *A History of the Guyanese Working People, 1881–1905*. Kingston: Heinemann Educational Books, 1981.

———. *How Europe Underdeveloped Africa*. London: Verso, 2018.

———. "Message to Afro-Jamaica Associations." *Bongo-Man* (1969): 14–17 (mimeograph in author's archive).

————. "Notes Towards a Popular History of Guyana." Guyana Symposium held in London, 23–24 October 1965 (Photocopy in author's archive).

————. "Some Implications of the Question of Disengagement from Imperialism." In *Socialism in Tanzania: An Interdisciplinary Reader: Policies*, vol. 2, edited by Lionel Cliffe and John S. Saul. Dar es Salaam: East Africa Publishing House, 1975.

————. *A Tribute to Walter Rodney: One Hundred Years of Development in Africa: Lectures Given at the University of Hamburg in Summer 1978.* Hamburg: University of Hamburg, 1984.

————. *Walter Rodney Speaks: The Making of an African Intellectual* (With an Introduction by Robert Hill and a Foreword by Howard Dodson). New Jersey: Africa World Press, 1990.

Roopnarine, Rupert. *The Sky's Wild Noise: Selected Essays.* Leeds: Peepal Tree Press, 2012.

Saul, John. "Radicalism and the Hill." In *Socialism in Tanzania-an Interdisciplinary Reader: Policies*, vol. 2, edited by Lionel Cliffe and John S. Saul. Dar es Salaam: East Africa Publishing House, 1975.

Shivji, Issa G., and Godwin R. Murunga, ed. *Where is Uhuru?: Reflections on the Struggle for Democracy in Africa.* Dar es Salaam: E & D Vision Publishing, 2009.

Ryan, Selwyn. *Eric Williams: The Myth and the Man.* Kingston: University of the West Indies Press, 2009.

Tetzlaff, Rainer, and Peter Lock, ed. *A Tribute to Walter Rodney: One Hundred Years of Development in Africa: Lectures Given at the University of Hamburg in Summer 1978.* Hamburg: University of Hamburg, 1984.

Trotz, Alissa, ed. *The Point is to Change the World: Selected Writings of Andaiye.* London: Pluto Press, 2020.

Wynter, Sylvia, and Demetrius L. Eudell, ed. *We Must Learn to Sit Down Together and Talk about a Little Culture: Decolonising Essays, 1967–1984.* Leeds: Peepal Tree Press, 2022.

Zeilig, Leo. *A Revolutionary for Our Time: The Walter Rodney Story.* Chicago: Haymarket Books, 2022.

ACKNOWLEDGEMENTS

All students of the work of Walter Rodney owe a debt of gratitude to Pat Rodney, his widow, who under extremely difficult circumstances raised their children and enabled their successful careers while she excelled in a career in public health. During the decades after Walter's assassination in 1980, she has preserved his legacy through the Walter Rodney Foundation and persisted in ensuring that a Commission of Enquiry investigate the death of her husband, which concluded that the Burnham government was responsible for his murder.

Thanks to my wife, Maureen Warner-Lewis, for her being a willing thinking companion and writing tutor. Thanks to Funso Aiyejina for inviting me to do this book, to the editor Susan Callum and to Rodney Worrell for valuable information on the much-neglected activists in Barbados in the 1960s and 1970s.

Printed in the USA
CPSIA information can be obtained
at www.ICGtesting.com
JSHW022220011124
R13792100001B/R137921PG72725JSX00001B/1